Ghosts of Seattle

Athena

Schiffer Publishing Ltd

4880 Lower Valley Road   Atglen, Pennsylvania   19310

Published by Schiffer Publishing Ltd.
4880 Lower Valley Road
Atglen, PA 19310
Phone: (610) 593-1777; Fax: (610) 593-2002
E-mail: Info@schifferbooks.com

For the largest selection of fine reference books on this and related subjects,
please visit our web site at
www.schifferbooks.com
We are always looking for people to write books on new and related subjects.
If you have an idea for a book please contact us at the above address.

This book may be purchased from the publisher.
Include $3.95 for shipping.
Please try your bookstore first.

You may write for a free catalog.

In Europe, Schiffer books are distributed by
Bushwood Books
6 Marksbury Ave.
Kew Gardens
Surrey TW9 4JF England
Phone: 44 (0) 20 8392-8585; Fax: 44 (0) 20 8392-9876
E-mail: info@bushwoodbooks.co.uk
Website: www.bushwoodbooks.co.uk
Free postage in the U.K., Europe; air mail at cost.

Copyright © 2007 by Athena
Library of Congress Control Number: 2007926905

Designed by Mark David Bowyer
Type set in Casablanca Antique / New Baskerville BT

ISBN: 978-0-7643-2687-5
Printed in China

Contents

Dedication:

I would like to dedicate this book to Chief Seattle. A brilliant man of strength and poetry far ahead of his time, Chief Seattle led his people in their darkest hours with a grace and dignity that makes him a powerful hero. This collection of stories is hereby dedicated to his memory.

"The sable braves, and fond mothers, and glad-hearted maidens, and the little children who lived and rejoiced here, and whose very names are now forgotten, still love these solitudes, and their deep fastnesses at eventide grow shadowy with the presence of dusky spirits. And when the last red man shall have perished from the earth and his memory among white men shall have become a myth, these shores shall swarm with the invisible dead of my tribe, and when your children's children shall think themselves alone in the field, the store, the shop, upon the highway or in the silence of the woods they will not be alone. In all the earth there is no place dedicated to solitude. At night, when the streets of your cities and villages shall be silent, and you think them deserted, they will throng with the returning hosts that once filled and still love this beautiful land. The white man will never be alone. Let him be just and deal kindly with my people, for the dead are not altogether powerless."

—Chief Seattle

Special Appreciation

I'd like to give my thanks and special appreciation to the following for all their help, support, and for sharing their stories with me;

A. J. Downey, founder of Seattle Ghost Hunters, for extensive help in finding sources and sharing stories.
Joe Teeples
Ross Allison
Jake from Private Eye Tours
Mercedes Yaeger, Administer of Creativity
Sheila Lyon
Seattle Ghost Hunters

W. S. P. I. R. (Washington State Paranormal Investigations and Research)
Darren Thompson, Director of Washington State Paranormal Investigations and Research.
Penny Truitt over at Bill Speidel's Underground tour
Midge Murky
Bonnie Kirby
A. G. H. O. S. T.

I'd also like to thank Dinah Roseberry for all her guidance and for encouraging me on my first adventure into the paranormal.

Thank you to my family for their support, and help; as well as the Valdez Crew who helped hold my sanity together—you guys are fabulous!

Special Appreciation and heartfelt thanks is also due to my dear friends in the Seattle area who let me stay in their home while I did research; Jeffrey Dean Croft and his lovely wife Sara—thank you so much for your generosity.

Foreword

My Views as an Author

A note on general paranormal research and the collection of folklore: While the science of the paranormal is still being 'tweaked,' it is undeniable that many unexplainable things do happen. Although many of these events are as of yet, without definition, that does not put them in the haunted category either. Science is the art of a repeatable explanation. It's human and tempting to desire an explanation to events which are fantastic, strange or just plain weird—but rushing to any conclusion can be more harmful than helpful to either the scientific cause or the foundation of a spiritual continuance. Because of this I have decided for purposes of my book, to tell these stories as I hear them; whether that be a first person or a five hundredth person accounting.

It is not my goal or aim to publish a collection of factual encounters of the spectral kind. In many cases I wasn't even able to trace the origin of the story, but most times the essence of the story and how often it is repeated and by whom—make it a worthy inclusion as it sets the stage for how the local residents of Seattle feel about their ghosts. I did not go to spooky locations with EMF detectors, or with any specialized equipment. I went with my digital camera and a notebook. I took no readings of any sort, nor did I attempt to judge in any way, the scientific or non-scientific validity of these areas.

To understand Seattle Ghosts, it is important to understand Seattle's history. Like most areas in North America, the settlement of towns and cities is often a dark and brutal saga. Seattle is no exception. When you think of a modern metropolis such as Seattle; famous for the Space Needle and being the birth place of Starbucks, Boeing, and Microsoft, you probably don't think of the civilization that existed on the land prior to the first explorers in 1792. The land Seattle now occupies was once maintained by Duwamish, Snoqualmie, Suquamish, and Nisqually tribes among a dozen or so others.

Named after Chief Seattle, a man of intense intelligence who helped lead his people in a tumultuous era, the city by his name is now a veritable trove of interesting paranormal stories; a fact I believe he wouldn't find the least bit unusual as he once was quoted, "Be just and deal kindly with my people, for the dead are not altogether powerless."

The Space Needle.

Later, his daughter, Princess Angeline, would be attributed with a curse said to kill anyone unfortunate enough to witness her specter. "Dead, did I say? There is no death, only a change of worlds."

Water

It's been reported that most recurring paranormal events take place near bodies of water; even submerged or underground lakes can contribute to a powerful haunting. An interesting study was done by a French immunologist, Jacques Benveniste, who claimed in a 1988 paper that he had discovered a scientic explanation for homeopathy. Water memory, is the theory that water can retain the 'memory' of any particle disolved in the liquid. While his research was termed "psuedoscience" by many, others caught on to the idea that once a "memory" of a solute has been formed in the water, the water will retain the properties of the substance and could be used for all manner of medical and scientific purposes. Whether this is a viable theory for the explination of repetative hauntings around water, I couldn't even guess. Yet I think it's something worth keeping in mind, as well as the works of Masaru Emoto, who's photographic journey and theories contained in the book, *Messages from Water* propose that water also has the capacity to absorb and retain emotions and intentions of people. The concept is interesting being that the human body is made up of 70% or more of water. For purposes of this book, I'd like to quote Masaru Emoto in his interview posted on www.beliefnet.com with Wendy Schuman:

> *"One of the first ones that was very surprising was our experiment with Fujiwara Dam in 1997. A Buddhist monk said he would go down to the water to pray for the water so we can purify the water. The reason why we were there was to get the sample of water before and after the prayer ceremony and see any difference in crystals. But even before we did [the experiment on] the crystals, right in front of our eyes the water started becoming clear. It was becoming different. Later on, a week later, we found out that a woman's body was found in the water; a day after that the killer was caught. When we came back to look at the crystals, the crystals before the prayer came up with an image that looked*

like a woman in agony. So we believe this is the woman's spirit that was actually projected. We looked at the water after the prayer and the crystal changed drastically. It was one of the most beautiful crystals we've ever seen."

Masaru Emoto's work is still being explored, but my interest increased after I knew I would be going to Seattle, which is a wet city most of the year, averaging thirty-six inches of rainfall. The Seattle area is also home to running ferries and floating bridges to much of the King County area in which the urban sprawl has crowded the Pacific Coast, inlets, islands, river, and lakes. In fact, the greater downtown area is sandwiched directly between Elliot Bay in Puget Sound on the Pacific Coast and Lake Washington, which is thirteen miles long.

When you factor in the works of Jacques Benveniste and Masaru Emoto, a search into the paranormal and unexplained stories of Seattle could very well dig up some interesting questions.

Whether you're reading this book for fun or for a greater interest in the unexplained, please keep in mind these two theories about water. Then once you add to this a hefty history of Indian struggles and American settlements, racial violence, Gold Rush greed, the bulldozing of Indian burial grounds, and the usual cases of impassioned murder, you get a fantastic stew of ghost stories.

While the stories I tracked down are far more recent than the deaths of Indians in land grabs and the body count left from communicable diseases brought in with the settlers, I suspect that if there is any great paranormal energy that contributes—these stories play a part in the level of intensity found in later hauntings which appear in structures built over Indian burial grounds and meeting areas, interestingly located within a few miles of a body of water.

Childhood

I set out to collect stories with what I hoped was an open mind. Through the course of my stay and research, I discovered a great many things about my concepts of the paranormal which hinged on two childhood experiences and a lifelong fascination with history and stories.

My first experience happened when I was perhaps twelve. I saw my uncle standing next to the car at a gas station in northern Utah where we were parked. I turned to my cousin who was sitting next to me and asked bewildered, "What's Uncle John doing up here?" She shrugged but didn't seem to see him standing plain as day next to the pump, so I let it drop. We drove home from the gas station, perhaps a fifteen minute drive, to arrive at the house in time for my aunt to rush through the door and pick up the ringing phone. It was my Uncle's wife calling to tell us that John had just suffered a major coronary and died on the operating table in southern Utah. He was legally dead for several minutes before being resuscitated.

My second and more frightening experience was during the same age period—twelve or thirteen. It was spring and I'd gone to a friend's house to play. Upon walking in, the hair on my arms and the back of my neck stood on end. I was suddenly paralyzed with fear, unable to breathe or move, and later I described to my dad, "It felt like someone was prying my chest open with a bar." I managed to see the face of another friend who'd come to the house with me and by the look on her face—she felt it, too. As soon as the feeling let up enough to move, we ran from the house to the park on the corner, where I cried. While being 'held,' I felt so full of despair, fear, and well… evil.

The girl who lived in the house was also about my age and when she'd heard we left the house at a run, she came to the park to explain and apologize. The manner in which she explained always sticks with me.

"Every year at about this time our house gets weird. We're just used to it. My older brother accidentally hung himself with the dog chain when he was trying to scare the babysitter about nine years ago. It was off the railing on the top floor and he was just playing around joking like he was going to kill himself. He made a mistake and he was too heavy for her to pull up by herself. You guys can come back, he won't hurt you."

I explained that what I felt was distinctly unfriendly. To which she continued,

"There's a story about the house also. My mom said when it used to be a house for girls up at the University, that they had a party in the 60's and a bunch of them died from overdosing. I don't know. I think there was also devil worshiping or something."

I walked with her back to the house, but just stepping on the lawn made me shiver and I ran away again. I didn't go back to her house for several months, although she claimed it only happened in the month of May. Later, I sat with my father and told him about the experience. His advice was this,

"Make your boundaries clear to all spirits. If you stay in your playground, they must respect your boundaries. If, however, you cross over in to their playground... the laws of protection do not apply anymore. Whatever you do, DON'T be afraid of them. What you fear, will find a way to get you. Don't be afraid of them."

He also gave me a chant, or a prayer-like command to use when I felt invaded or threatened.

I never asked my dad how he knew these things. Maybe I worried that he'd tell me he just made it up, in which case the strength I took from his words when I was a little girl, would evaporate. All I know is that I said the chants frequently over the next couple of years and as I passed out of puberty—I haven't had a similar experience. Since that time I've been able to convince myself of every possible explanation, but most often, I land back on the idea that I was just a kid and therefore susceptible to emotional fancy and over-reaction. In the last fifteen years I've also developed a skeptical outer casing that I hope, to some degree, is balanced with the interest of being proved wrong, or enough of an open mind to be able to see more of the overall picture. The possibilities of the paranormal are endless, and I'm game to see where some of those possibilities lead; at the same time, I maintain that my most solid interest is in the folklore of the area. I believe it's worth noting what stories persist, which accountings of the paranormal are considered worthy of repetition by the locals of the city. I believe these stories of ghosts and of the myths and experiences of the other realm say a great deal about the citizens of a specific city. It gives a glimpse into the foundations of their interests and their hopes as well as litmus of what parts of their history with which they have the most resonance. At the very least, ghosts stories can be entertaining, there's something about the fright factor that tempts us all, whether it's a trip to the theatre for the latest slasher, or a night of camping where stories are gleefully told around a fire.

So much of our culture remains oral. Though the light-speed evolution of the communication age has altered the landscape of traditional oral tellings, there is still an element of pop culture that requires the social experience of "passing the story." As with most urban legends, myths, and folklore—one must expect a certain percentage of mutation from telling to telling. However the alterations shift the details of a story, the base is often intact. This it the gold. This is why we happily sit around a fire with smores and listen. We want the diversion of entertainment, but we also secretly want the challenge of puzzling out the grain of truth. We want to add our own twists, our own opinions, and our own explanations. We thrill in the adrenaline of the experience of listening, and the excitement of the retelling. We are still oral historians to this day, perhaps a little different than our fathers and mothers were, but still the enjoyment of history in all its tainted and fantastic glory intrigues us.

So it is with this in mind that I set about finding the treasures of storytelling in Seattle. Are there ghosts? Maybe. Does it matter? Probably. But to me, their existence matters not as much as exploring the possibility that there is such a medium, a food perhaps, which ghost stories require to survive. A social eco-structure that acts as an amniotic fluid of sorts to incubate the stories themselves, and provide a rich and glittering substance for the modern imagination.

Seattle's Ghosts

Suspension of Disbelief

"Who here on this tour believes in ghosts?" Jake asked.

I turned in the seat to glance at the other passengers in the van, curious as to who would fess up and who would demure. The couple in the very back, perhaps in their late forties, had no hesitation in admitting that they fully and enthusiastically believed in ghosts. They'd even brought a small EMF detector. The family in the center shrugged and mumbled. The young woman looked at her father, the father looked at the mother and she lifted up her palms; whereupon the father and daughter both lifted up their palms.

Then there was me. Contracted to write a book on ghosts in Seattle, not really knowing anything about the paranormal, I sat in the passenger seat up front of the fifteen passenger van on a haunted tour of Seattle. All eyes were on me as I wondered for a moment what to say. I could say no, but that wouldn't be true—I'd had at least two unexplainable experiences in my life. I couldn't say yes, because although those experiences where currently unexplained, that doesn't provide any kind of scientific proof of the paranormal. I couldn't honestly say either way, but part of the reason I accepted the Seattle ghosts gig was to find out. What do I really believe?

"I'm on the fence," I said aloud. While thinking to myself, 'but the fence leans toward no—I don't believe in ghosts.'

Jake smiled in a way that made it seem like she'd just accepted the challenge. Jake is in fact a woman in her mid forties, beautiful and while talkative and animated about the topic of the paranormal, she quickly becomes unassuming and soft when asked about any area not pertaining to the dead. I'd spoken to her on the phone while making my reservation for the tour and my imagination conjured something entirely different than what greeted me at the pickup site. I'd imagined an eccentric gothic rollover or even a middle-aged woman in safari gear with a backpack full of infrared camera gear and other paraphernalia designed to prove the existence of ghosts. What I hadn't expected was someone who could pass as a soccer mom in Banana Republic khaki's and a white summer jacket with blonde hair and an easy smile.

We pulled out onto the crowed streets of Downtown Seattle. Jake switched on the headpiece she wore that connected to the speaker system in the van so everyone could hear her talk as we made our way to First Street. We passed the Space Needle, the Music Project and the Monorail. Being that Seattle was not my home turf, I was happy to have someone else do the driving as well as give a little history about the area not considered paranormal in nature. Jake was born in Seattle and knew things a college guide, or an "import" as most true Seattle residents would call a non-local, wouldn't know. Street names that have changed over the years, neighborhood lines redrawn and buildings that have been moved.

The Chelsea Apartments are located on Queen Ann Hill where some side streets are a collision of old world and new with patches of cobblestone and brickwork peeking out from poorly laid asphalt. The cumbersome van bounced over what some would call imperfections, but I thought of as charming glimpses of the past. The roads are also some of the steepest I've seen—worse even than San Francisco. I clutched the rubber grip on my door.

Undaunted, Jake continued to talk about the area and the breathtaking mansions that were once the residences for the wealthy elite of early Seattle. I knew I'd really like her when she sadly commented on a vacant lot where bulldozers were parked amidst ruble. "That used to be a fabulous building. They knocked it down to build condos—they call it progress."

To say Seattle is 'hilly' would be a vast understatement. In fact, I would venture to call it "undulating." What it is now though, is infinitely more traversable than when it was originally settled. The area was so rugged when the city's founding father's tried to put down their roots, that endless "upgrades" were required to make the land functional for a metropolis. The Denny Regrade Project in 1898 is probably the most famous of these ventures which required removing a mountain and dumping the earth in Elliott Bay, thereby flattening the plats and extending the shore with clean landfill. Denny Hill as it used to be, overlooked Elliott Bay with enough height to see any enemy coming for miles, so it isn't a wonder that the local natives put their ancestral burial ground up where the view was breathtaking and the spirits could protect the land.

As we passed through the Queen Ann neighborhood, Jake explained, "They worked around the clock to flatten Denny Hill which used to be an Indian burial ground. Residents started complaining about the exhumed bodies of Indians and settlers alike, so the graveyard shift was founded to exhume and remove the dead when residents were fast asleep, thereby sparing them the gory details."

The etymology of graveyard shift is sketchy, but graveyard watch was a nautical term used by sailors in the 1890s to describe the hours between midnight and dawn. It's of interest to me that ghost hunters also remark that the best time to witness paranormal activity is between midnight and four am. Whether this is because the world slows down and becomes quiet, and the spirits are more noticeable (although they are always present), or if they specifically choose that time of day to become active—no one is sure. Yet it's worth mentioning that during the graveyard shift, the ghosts are more likely to come out and play.

The Chelsea is an adorable building that once served as an upscale hotel in the days of yore when a vacation meant more than a two week blip. Back when steamer trunks and month long voyages were taken as journeys to broaden the horizons for a month or two at a time, the Chelsea served to home many a traveler. Eventually, grander and more elaborate hotels were erected in Seattle and the once lively Chelsea was turned into low cost apartments much to the horror of local residents.

As Jake tells the story, there were two noteworthy incidents in the Chelsea Apartments. The first being a woman who was so tired of her husband being abusive that she waited for him to pass out drunk before tying a noose around his throat and folding the Murphy bed into the wall thereby hanging him inside the bed.

The second story claims that a young man and his buddies went out drinking and came home falling down drunk. At some point in the evening, the young man fell and hit his head but refused to go to the hospital although he was suffering from a concussion. The next morning his body was found, and although there were signs of a struggle and much blood, the case was closed due to the cause of death being a traumatic head wound.

Jake's voice took on a deep and rhythmic tone as she described the stories and the subsequent haunting. "The landlords have difficulty renting the apartment, and no one stays for long. The people who lived in the corner apartment there had a cat that absolutely refused to enter one of the rooms even when a can of tuna was set out, which the cat loved."

Jake took the van to several locations and during the three hour tour I watched with fascination as the other members of the group seemed to catch her enthusiasm for the subject material. It was an affirmation to me that there's a great deal of interest in the topic of the paranormal, and yet few people have the courage to venture into a territory that is either fearful, or as many others would call it—crazy. It was during this first tour with Jake that I found a fountain of curiosity to explore the stories of this area and to discover the connection between the urban legends and the people who repeat them, as well and the myths and those who believe. It became apparent that the true story would not simply be the deaths and the hauntings, but the people who shiver with excitement or anxiety at the mere mention of a spirit. It would be the people who ask questions and retell accounts with hushed voices and white knuckles, and luckily for me—Seattle was loaded with both.

The Arctic Club

One of the more conspiracy-wracked and heated ghost stories is the death of United States Congressman, Marion A. Zioncheck. Although many say suicide, there are those who will quickly speak out that it was murder. This accounts for his unrest and the subsequent hauntings on the fifth floor of the Arctic Club, which is now the Arctic Hotel on the corner of Third Street and Cherry in downtown. An architecturally beautiful building with easy-to-recognize walruses on the exterior of the third floor, the Arctic Club is currently being remodeled to become the Arctic Hotel.

Marion Zioncheck was born in Poland and immigrated with his parents to the newly rebuilt Seattle. He earned a law degree while causing a stir at the University of Washington as a Democratic Party and Washington Commonwealth Federation (WCF) leader, which helped him get elected to Congress in 1932. He served as a Democrat and was particularly affected by the division of classes, being that he was the son of immigrants and having worked his way through college, he became a champion to the lower class.

It's said that during his days at school he would develop his political platform, which would eventually land him squarely in the category of a radical reformist. Seattle's political history is rife with corruption, and very few old timers were said to appreciate the upstart young Zioncheck.

Congressman Zioncheck supported Roosevelt's New Deal policies which were designed to improve the United States Economy during the Depression, but he was also known for his schoolboy antics. Most famously, he's remembered for driving on the lawn of the White House, and drunken dancing in the Washington, D. C. fountain. He was often accompanied on his late night escapades by his wife, Rubeye Louise Nix.

Walrus embellishments on the exterior of the Arctic Club.

Right:
Congressman Zioncheck falls to his death on Third Street from the fifth floor window of the Arctic Club.

When his friend, Warren G. Magnuson, filed to run against him in the 1936 election, Zioncheck was reported to be despondent. Six days later he was said to have penned a suicide note;

"My only hope in life was to improve the conditions of an unfair economic system."

The press claims he then threw himself from the window of his fifth floor office in the Arctic Club Building while his brother-in-law watched in disbelief, as he hit the pavement on Third Street in front of the car where his wife Rubeye sat waiting.

Magnuson succeeded Zioncheck and stories were evenly divided between murder and suicide. Those of the lower class, to whom Zioncheck had become a champion, simply couldn't believe that a man as firm in his convictions of reform could simply give up.

Over the years, the stories of the fifth floor haunting include: Strange noises in the elevator, the elevator door opening and closing of its own accord at the fifth level, and one report of a woman feeling as though she were not alone in the elevator though not feeling threatened or in danger.

Seattle Ghost Hunters informed me that there have been sightings of orbs and unusual EMF readings on the fifth floor.

We may never know whether he committed suicide or whether he was pushed, but the family of Marion Zioncheck still continues the search for answers, even running a website to gather information from witnesses who may have see anything that night, seventy years ago.

Comet Lodge Cemetery

Comet Lodge Cemetery rests on the southern part of Beacon Hill overlooking the Georgetown area. The lore surround the Cemetery is difficult to prove, but the stories are fascinating, some of which could be right out of the movie *Poltergeist*.

As it was told to me, the cemetery was once a seven-acre plat. On those seven acres, the city maintained a section for the local hospital deaths, many of whom were children and infants. The story gets confusing when five of the seven acres are sold off and the headstones are lost or removed. At some point down the road, the city "forgets" where the plat lines are drawn and the developer who buys the five-acre chunk builds twelve houses on the edge of what he assumes is only a two-acre cemetery. The houses are built in the 1970s and the families who move in to said homes begin to notice strange things, mostly involving children.

Comet Lodge Cemetery.

One story claims that a woman installed an expensive glass display case for her porcelain doll collection. The case was complete with special lighting and a sturdy lock. Being very proud of her dolls the woman would check her case at night to be sure it was locked, and the next morning she would wake to discover her dolls scattered about the room as though they'd been "played with."

Another family had a young boy who was an only child. They frequently admonished the boy for leaving his toys scattered around the house, even though he claimed not to have played with any of them. The parents began forcing him to clean up before bed. He'd stack the toys in a box and, upon waking the next morning, the toys were all over the house, on every level and even the stairs. The kid continued to get into trouble until he mentioned that a strange boy would come into his room at night and sit on the edge of his bed. When the parents asked who the new boy was, the son replied, "I don't know. He's dressed funny and he's older, I think he thinks he's watching out for me."

Tragically, the two acres of cemetery land went uncared for until it had virtually become choked with weeds and blackberries. So many years passed in this condition that many people in the area didn't even know it was a graveyard. When the city put out notice that it planned to build a dog park on the "vacant lot," a longtime resident, who actually knew what lay hidden under the thorny bramble, came forward to protest.

An emergency rehabilitation was planned whereupon volunteers worked day and night for a week to uncover as many headstones as possible to keep the city from bulldozing the land. Thankfully, it worked—unfortunately, many of the residents had no idea they'd been living next to a cemetery and several moved away. This however seemed to confirm to many of the owners of the twelve houses, that there was in fact a valid reason for the hauntings.

Comet Lodge Cemetery is now a beautiful spot of tree-covered land nestled in a small neighborhood where many reports of unusual, but harmless, encounters circulate such as: orbs, the laughter of children, and a pervading sense of being watched.

When I first went to the Comet Lodge Cemetery, I decided I would come back at dusk and spend the night. I rented a motel room a few miles away, and each night I would pack my video camera, my thermos of coffee, and my sleeping gear. And each night, I'm ashamed to admit—I found excuses not to venture into the graveyard alone. It took me weeks to admit to myself that it wasn't really that I'd stayed at the seedy motel because I wanted to watch a rerun episode of *Law and Order*, but that I was actually... get this... scared.

It was the first time my research made a noticeable ding in my composure and my beliefs about the supernatural, but it wouldn't be the last.

Later, as I was telling AJ Downey from Seattle Ghost Hunters about my personal revelation pertaining to a fear I didn't even know I had, she laughed.

A pile of headstones in Comet Lodge Cemetery. No one knows exactly where the plots for these headstones are located.

"We went out there one night and set up our gear—we took a nun with us." AJ laughed again. "We didn't see a single thing and we'd gone out there to investigate the reports of iridescent children playing in the graveyard at dusk."

Joe Teeples, another member of Seattle Ghost Hunters and a published writer on the topic of the paranormal, was standing nearby and chimed in, "You were going to go out there alone? Number one rule in ghost hunting is…"

"Never go out alone!" AJ and Joe finished simultaneously while looking at me with stern frowns.

"Beside the obvious reasons of a young woman out at night alone," Joe continued. "You should never go out hunting by yourself because firstly, if you get into trouble, there's no one to help. Secondly, if you see anything—you need a witness."

Needless to say I felt like a monumental idiot, these things had honestly not even occurred to me.

"But let me mention AGAIN, being a young woman alone at night is never a good idea under any circumstance." Joe leveled a fatherly gaze in my direction and raised his eyebrows.

AJ piped in, "Except, I guess if you were alone in a graveyard at night, the odds of a creep bothering you are pretty slim being that if you're in the graveyard—he's likely too chicken to mess with you."

Joe laughed. "True enough. If your there, he'll probably think twice because you look too hardcore to tamper with."

Joe and AJ from the Seattle Ghost Hunters were a fabulous help and certainly knew their stuff. I left our meeting feeling silly, knowing full well I was out of my element, as proof of my intention to visit the cemetery alone despite my fear and backing out. The whole adventure opened my eyes to a new part of my inner psychology in terms of what I thought about ghosts, and the sudden awareness that I might have bitten off more than I could safely chew in accepting a gig about the supernatural underground of Seattle.

As I went on to continue my research, I could no longer pretend that I was unaffected by the stories I found. Whether one factors in spirits or not, I believe it does something to your mental process when you stand in the very spot someone died a horrific and painful death. Just the knowledge of another human being suffering gives a sliver of empathy to the thought process that agony might have repercussions that lead to unexplainable phenomenon. Once a sliver of possibility is given to the supernatural, you are wide open to the tricks of your imagination and to the emotional backlash of sympathetic involvement.

I could no longer play at the "no such thing as ghosts" because I'd allowed a sliver of doubt to enter, thereby igniting imagination and adding fuel to the need to seek out the truth of the stories.

The Harvard Exit Theatre

I met Ross Allison, founder of A.G.H.O.S.T (Amateur Ghost Hunters Of Seattle Tacoma), at the Harvard Exit Theatre. Ross is also a co-author for the book *Ghostology 101* along with Joe Teeples. The Harvard Exit was built in 1925 and given landmark status in 1979, although the Women's Century Club was founded in 1891. As the original meeting place of the Women's Century Club, Seattle's early feminist movement, it is said to be the most interesting paranormal resource in the city. The building was converted into a two-screen theatre in the 1980s and still does enough business despite local giants to keep the doors open to the public.

Walking in to the main lobby, I was immediately won over by the original brass light fixtures and gold framed paintings that date to the turn of the century. There's a grand piano in front of the antique fireplace, and an old movie projector sitting on display near the concession stand. It's not your average movie theatre; in fact it's a pleasant time warp to the 1920s despite a few modern additions.

Ross was waiting for me in a top hat and brocade coat. He leaned against the concessions counter with an old-school walking stick waiting expectantly for my arrival. A Ghost leads haunted tours of Capitol Hill beginning at the Harvard Exit, several days a week. I just happened to be there on a slow day and took the tour alone, which provided me with plenty of opportunities to ask questions.

The reports circling the Harvard Exit Theatre usually mention a woman in an early-century gown in a floral print. Her hair is drawn up in a bun and she's seen wandering the lobby, or sitting in a chair by the fire reading a book. Most people who've seen her claim that, as they try to speak with her, she becomes transparent or vanishes. The most popular theory of this particular ghost is that it is the specter of Bertha Knight Landes.

In 1921, Bertha Knight Landes was the President of the Seattle Federation of Women's Clubs. She was a member of the Women's Century

The Harvard Exit Theatre lobby and fireplace.

Club that met where the Harvard Exit now shows art flicks and third-run movies. In 1926, Bertha was elected as Seattle's first female Mayor and served one term. Most noted for her "municipal housekeeping" and encouraging women to take the vote, many people believe that it's only natural that Bertha would persist in looking out for the Women's Century Club, which continues to meet in front of the fireplace eighty years later.

It's said that once, when an employee of the theatre entered the lobby to turn out a lamp, the figure of a woman matching the description of Bertha Knight Landes rose up out of a chair where she was presumably reading, smiled at the girl, then turned off the lamp and walked past the astonished employee whereupon the ghost evaporated.

Workers at the theatre also say that there have been times when the building was unlocked in the morning; the chairs have been arranged in a semi-circle in front of the fireplace... as if the Century Club was holding midnight meetings. When the modern women's club is questioned, they deny having been in the building.

Other accounts involve the fireplace. It used to be tradition that a fire was lit every night in the hearth, but extinguished before the building was locked down for the evening. Many employees have claimed that when the theatre was opened the next day, there was a fresh fire already blazing in the fireplace.

Whether the "caretaker" of the lobby is Bertha Landes, we'll never know. I think, however, that it brings a great deal of comfort to the occupants and employees of the building that it might indeed be her. There's no small amount of pride in the accomplishments of Seattle's first female mayor, suffragist, and overall motherly figure of the early century. Bertha Knight Landes was far ahead of her time, and most of the people I've spoken to are proud to call her a "long time (and still) resident" of Seattle. Bertha died in 1943. She was seventy-five years old.

Ross took me down the stairs to the basement. Mostly unfinished and poorly lit, if lit at all, and smelling of dust and mildew, the basement gave me the creeps. While I didn't feel threatened or even have the heebie-jeebies per se, I certainly felt the history and the weight of the building on my awareness.

There were several places where three or four stairs led a little further down. It felt like two stories and I became a little disoriented. The first main level, which would be directly under the lobby, appeared to be a storage area. Planks and miscellaneous items were stacked in haphazard piles. Remembrances of many decades were cast aside in the underground space. Wingback reading chairs from the 1950s, a bicycle from the 1960s, and a popcorn machine that appeared to be from the late 80s.

"The only reason anyone would come down here, is to hook up the hoses for the soda machines for the concessions." Ross pointed at the rack of syrup boxes and hoses fed through the ceiling.

I found my way through the Harvard Exit Theatre basement using the flash on my digital camera.

Two separate doors led to abandoned restrooms with aged plumbing fixtures and debris. In places where there was little or no light, I used the flash of my digital camera to get around.

Next I followed him to the boiler room which went down another set of rickety stairs and into a space that plastered me with spider webs. To my shame, I squeaked like a girl, swiping the sticky threads and shivering.

"I guess that comes with the territory," I said.

"It sure does," he agreed.

I took several shots of the boiler room, but whether it was the spider silk or some other feeling, I wanted to go back upstairs.

"Are you feeling anything?" He asked.

Abandoned restrooms in the basement of the Harvard Exit Theatre gave me the creeps.

"Well, yeah, but I think it's just the weirdness of the place. Plus I haven't gotten much sleep lately, and I've felt like I'm getting the flu lately, so I have to factor those things in when I feel weird on these scenes."

"Yes, I believe you do." He nodded.

"Especially, the fatigue, as I think your melatonin levels can sure mess with what you think you're feeling."

"How so?"

"Well, I know this is silly, but I've been pulling late nights at my computer. Not sleeping enough, and last night I got really tired so I thought I'd go take a cold shower to wake myself up." I sighed. "When I came back to my room, my bed was turned down, and a fortune from a cookie I'd eaten was on the floor by my bed, rather than in the window where I thought I'd left it."

"Really."

"I asked my room mates if they'd done it, but they all swore they hadn't. One of them even said, 'Well, haven't you been writing ghosts stories? Maybe you should get some sleep.'" I shrugged. "Ultimately, I decided that I'd probably done it myself as some subconscious effort to encourage myself to go to bed. I really did need the sleep. So for instances like that—I really think you should take into consideration how your overall body and mind is feeling at the time you have an 'incident.' Although I don't remember turning my bed down, I can't rule out the possibility that I had."

Ross didn't comment on my story, but we headed up the stairs where I felt better upon seeing sunlight. From the main floor, we climbed up stairs with what appeared to be the original banisters and spindles. Beautiful dark wood with a polish that spoke volumes about how many people had run their hands over the railing in the last eighty years.

On the third floor of the Harvard Exit Theatre, there is an auditorium, a projection booth, a set of restrooms, and two separate and open meeting rooms. The large windows of the top floor are shaded by outside trees which also helps buffer the noise of Capitol Hill. Even though there was a movie going on the auditorium next to the rooms, I couldn't hear it.

The third floor rooms are sometimes used as meeting spaces for groups such as A.G.H.O.S.T.

The stories of the Harvard Exit Theatre's third floor are often told and retold with a great sense of pride by the residents of the area and the employees. Many of the ghost hunting groups of the area have done their own independent investigations in an attempt to collaborate these popular stories: A woman in Victorian garb is often seen standing on the landing of the stairs—if her strange dress doesn't draw attention, the fact that she has no hands or face, certainly does.

The landing between the second and third floors where reports of a woman in Victorian dress is observed without hands or a face.

People have reported hearing voices, laughter, footsteps, and crying when they are alone. There are also persistent reports of a strong presence. A sense of "unwelcomness." It's of interest to note, these reports have mostly been mentioned by men. There's a belief that an essence of what some might call a "thought form" lingers from the original Women's Century Club which exists today to protect women from the male sex.

There have been reports of women in early 1900s-style gowns milling around the top floor.

Some reports claim to have seen a woman hanging on the landing, but stories as they are repeated also claim the woman was hanging in the bathroom where she committed suicide. However, I have been unable to find any records of a hanging or suicide at the Harvard Exit Theatre.

Employees say that, sometimes when they come to work; things are rearranged, primarily in the projection booth.

One popular story that is often told is of the projection booth operator who came to work and discovered that the movie was running already—but the booth was locked from the inside. By the time they managed to get inside, the booth was empty.

A "portly" middle-aged man has been spotted in old-fashioned clothing and seems to be the remnants of a story whereupon the Harvard Exit Theatre was built on the lot where a home had once existed that housed the grisly murder of a man.

My personal favorite is story of one of the theater's early managers. Once night he was closing up and heard a noise on the third floor. He raced up to catch the intruder, following the noise to the emergency exit that was still closing. The manager grabbed the door in an attempt to catch what he evidently thought would be a teenager or a trouble maker. The door refused to open. He put his weight against the door but was only able to make it move marginally. He became angry, thinking that someone was playing tug of war with him. Then the door suddenly gave and the manager found himself on the empty landing outside. There wasn't anyone on the metal stairwell which is clearly visible for three flights—and being that it is an emergency exit, there isn't a handle on the outside of the door.

The fire escape door has no handle on the outside.

The stories Ross told me were all well documented favorites. I'd heard most of them before, and while I enjoyed the retelling, I couldn't help but be more impressed by the spectacularly charming environment than the somewhat creepifying hauntings.

The Seattle Ghost Hunters did a preliminary investigation in which they found enough curiosities to warrant a more thorough study. Upon their arrival, they took several pictures, and managed to catch a few small orbs. One of the men on the team, Joe, also felt as though he'd been hit in the chest upon entering the room.

I was able to view a picture on their website that shows an interesting "vortex" in front of AJ as she's walking through the main theatre. It was particularly remarkable to me as it looked as though there was a strip of white running through her face while the rest of her upper body appears to be seen through a funhouse mirror. There's definitely some sort of distortion.

Seattle Ghost Hunters also took EMF readings in the ladies room while asking questions of a 'yes or no' nature, such as; "Would you like the men to leave?" They report getting slight responses to this experiment.

Their overall assessment of the theatre is that there is definitely a strange sense of oppressiveness in the building and enough anomalies to ensure the need for a more in-depth session. It's my personal belief, however, that regardless of what the research finds, the Harvard Exit Theatre formerly known as the Women's Century Club will remain a favorite haunted location wherein the stories of Bertha Landes and others will have a comfortable and prolific lifespan, simply because the residents of Seattle wish it to be so.

Capitol Hill

Capitol Hill was originally founded in hopes of Seattle becoming the capital of Washington State. Unfortunately, Olympia had already been chosen as the center of government for the Evergreen State.

The hill has a rich history of intrigue, as most places of commerce do. The tour, guided by Ross, took me past several locations of misadventure.

After the Harvard Exit Theatre, we walked down Broadway to the QFC. "Back in the 80s, a kid overdosed in the upstairs restroom. You can't see it from here, but there used to be an upper floor where the bathrooms were. When they were remodeling it some years later to turn it into this QFC, the workers reported that their tools would move around. Electrical fixtures went on and off and so on."

"Are there any documented interviews or research?" I asked.

He adjusted his top hat. "No, just what people repeat."

We crossed the street and ventured up a smaller street to a stunning apartment building. Built in the early 1900s, the building was fairly drowning in ivy and wrought iron. Old stone decorations and a quaint courtyard made for a very ghostly setting.

"This site is new on the tour. I'm still trying to get more information."

"I totally understand. So it's haunted?"

"Well, the story goes that once a newlywed couple moved into the apartment that faces out. Soon after they arrived, the woman began have extremely—uh—erotic dreams."

"Nice. Now you've got my undivided attention."

He laughed. "So she couldn't understand it. It seemed that every night her dreams were visited by a man whom she claimed was someone she wasn't even attracted to, and yet he could manage to make her respond exactly how he wanted."

"Hmm, sounds sketchy," I added.

"Yeah, and some nights the couple reported that they couldn't sleep from all the noises of—uh, lovemaking coming from the wall, but it was the exterior wall of the building."

Haunting? Or a newly wedded wife unsatisfied with her husband and fantasizing about another man?

The courtyard of the newlyweds.

Further up the road, we turned onto 15th where we stood across the street from an old firehouse which has recently been converted into 15th Avenue Video.

The front of the building still has the original stall doors but since the renovation, rows of shelving and display cases prevent the doors from opening. The adorable red brick firehouse has been noted for housing the occasional shadowy form, swinging interior doors, and one account of a man in old-style clothing striding across the main room and vanishing.

I went to the counter and introduced myself to a young man. He had spiked hair, multiple tattoos, and seemed unimpressed with my, *I'm writing a book on ghost stories* introduction.

"Have you noticed anything strange or unusual since you've been working here?"

He sighed as if put upon to reply, "No."

"Can I talk to the owner or maybe someone I can ask questions?"

"Hey, Steve. They want to know about ghosts," he shouted to the other guy only a few feet away.

"Tell them to call May," Steve shouted back.

I resisted the urge to cover my ears. "Do you have a business card?" I asked.

Spiky-tattoo-guy sighed again, "Yeah."

We left the building, followed by several odd glances and more than a couple of eye rolling shrugs.

However much the boys at the firehouse were disinterested in talking to us—the waitress and bartender at The Canterbury, just up the block, made the whole trip worth while. The Canterbury looks like a tavern from the 1700s. White-washed exterior walls and dark-wood trim with wrought iron decorations make it just the sort of place one would expect to find ghosts. Upon walking in, I was immediately impressed with the antique, stained-glass panels which gave the light a level of ambiance conducive to storytelling.

Ross and I approached the waitress's station in the rear of the restaurant near the bar. We met Beth.

"I'm collecting stories on ghosts for the Seattle area…" I began, but before I could even finish my pitch she became animated.

She leaned into the counter blurting, "Oh, my god. I have a great story. I saw a ghost here one night and it freaked me out!"

"Really?" Ross asked, leaning into the bar.

Beth perched her ticket booklet and rag on a stack of menus. "Yeah, really. There's an old rumor that several years back, a guy got shot in the face out here on the street. Well I didn't pay much attention to the rumor cuz, well, it's old, and one night it was really late and I thought I was alone behind the bar—except for Jimmy who was in the back. Anyway, I glance up and through the columns, I can see the mirror hanging on the wall in the next room. I noticed someone in the reflection so I craned my neck a little to see them better and I swear the guy was missing the bottom have of his face!"

Beth put her hands up to her chin and shuddered.

"What happened?" I asked.

"Then I started screaming. I screamed for Jimmy to get his ass up to the bar, and the half-face guy just disappeared. I guess the ghost had thought I was alone too, and didn't want to meet Jimmy."

She shivered. "I don't close alone ever. I mean before that, we never closed alone but *after* that, I'm damn sure I never close up by myself. We try to make sure no one is ever in the building alone."

"Have you seen anything since?" I asked.

"No. That was pretty much it." She added with a sigh of relief. "Wait, let me ask some of the regulars." She ambled over to the bar that was already beginning to fill up at 6:30 pm. "Hey, any of you guys ever seen any ghosts around here, or anything weird?"

The patrons shook their heads. Some glanced around at their fellows before shrugging and frowning a 'no'.

"How about you guys?" Beth asked a table of college-aged kids. "You guys know of any haunted spots for these people to check out?"

The kids shrugged and shook their heads. As I pulled out my camera to take a picture of the mirror Beth had mentioned, one of the kids… a young man perhaps twenty-five asked softly, "Have you been to the Harvard Exit Theatre yet?"

The mirror is said to have reflected the specter of a man missing half his face.

"Yes, actually, we just came from there," I answered.

"What about Pike Place Market?" asked the girl across the table. "Pike's is haunted, too."

"Yeah..." I looked at them again and suddenly they were talking over each other to point us in the direction of places they'd heard were haunted. Lake View Cemetery. Highway 101. The Neptune Theatre.

I smiled, thinking it might just be a second for most people to get over the shock of having the topic of ghosts brought up in social conversation, but once they get over the shock... most people have stories or a place or at least an interest in the paranormal.

We talked with the kids who were having coffee and fries, before I took several pictures of the interior and the stained-glass panels. As we left, I said, "Strange. If I were walking by this place, I would think it seems just like the kind of place that would be haunted. But I likely never would have gone in, because I never would have believed that tiny little unmarked brown door on the side was the entrance."

The stroll up 15th was leisurely and full of beautiful Victorian and Craftsman-style homes worthy of a television special and likely stuffed to the rafters with stories of ghosts. Entering into Volunteer Park we came to the famous red brick water tower.

"This water tower has a ghost story that is often repeated," Ross explained. "I haven't been able to verify it obviously, but it's fun nonetheless."

"Go on," I encouraged while wandering around the wide base of the 1907 structure. As I watched Ross slip into storytelling mode, I realized that he truly loved his work. (Honestly, I thought, it takes a very secure man to wear a top hat and a 1870s silver brocade coat in public— or a guy who really loves to tell stories!) He swung his cane with a rhythm that matched his singsong voice, which lowered as he reached the climax of the tale.

"Women claim to hear footsteps coming down the stairs behind them, when they know they're alone and that there was no one at the top. There has also been a claim of a large man in overalls, like work overall's at the window up at the top, but when people go up the stairs, there's no one there."

The water tower on Capitol Hill.

I took a closer look at the bricks. Many of them looked to have been melted, some even had a glassy sheen and rounded corners as though they'd been glazed.

"This place was built in 1907 right?" I asked.

"Yeah, I think so," Ross said rubbing a spot on his forehead where his top hat appeared to have left an indent.

"Is it possible that these bricks are from the great fire? I mean, it makes sense that they would reuse them from 1889, being that at the time, all bricks were being shipped in from San Francisco. So wouldn't it make sense to just reuse some of the burned bricks rather than pay for shipping on new stone just for a water tower?"

I felt elated for a moment. Maybe this ghost hunting thing wouldn't be so hard, sort of a detective story. I imagined briefly that I'd have to start dressing the part, maybe get a trench coat and a start smoking in the rain with a fedora.

Ross shrugged, "I guess."

All my thoughts of cigarettes and ghost stakeouts vanished in a blink. I felt the enthusiasm for my inquisitive sleuthing pop like an overfilled balloon.

"Oh."

Not related to the water tower, but a curious side-trek into the topic of bricks in Seattle, I also heard a tale in passing from two different individuals about the 1906 San Francisco earthquake. It seems there is a legend in circulation that a ship leaving the Bay Area after the great quake shoveled rubble from collapsed buildings into the ballast. When the ship docked in Seattle, passengers disembarked complaining of "strange happenings" and overall uncomfortableness. The ballast stones were dumped, only to have it revealed that human remains from the earthquake were mixed in with the broken bricks and crumbled mortar.

"Would you like to see the next stop on the tour?"

"Sure," I said, and returned to my modern not-so-romantic version of story collecting with blisters on my heels from my tennis shoes and an aching back from lugging my tripod and camera gear around in a sack.

Melted bricks make up the water tower.

About fifty yards away from the water tower, we came to the entrance for Volunteer Park, a rich expanse of green, lush trees with a magnificent view of the city.

"Back when the city was settled, they went through several renovations of graveyards. Sometimes people were buried three times. Interred, dug up, moved, and interred again until the city finally stopped moving the graveyards around."

Ross began moving again and we walked past the Seattle Asian Art Museum, where the famous statue of the Black Hole Sun overlooks the reservoir and a magnificent scenic view of downtown Seattle. His cane tapped against the sidewalk each time his left foot touched down and I found myself unintentionally matching his tempo.

Entrance to Volunteer Park.

"When the city finally decided to stop moving bodies around, the park was established, but many people are sure that the park holds a few bodies that were never found," he said.

"So the moral of the story is 'Don't bring your cadaver dog on a picnic to Volunteer Park.'" I replied.

. He coughed a short laugh and continued with the story, "Some people claim to have seen a naked man running through the trees over there. They say he was battered and bloody, but he was never found, and no one ever reported a man of his description missing."

Volunteer Park is sided by Lakeview Cemetery which is the resting place for most of Seattle's founding fathers and the cast of characters that gives the city its colorful history. Founded in 1887, as cemeteries go, I would easily say this one passes for picturesque. Although Chief Seattle and Princess Angeline are said to have been buried in Lakeview, the most visited and famous headstones are those of Bruce Lee and his son Brandon.

"This graveyard has a very popular story about a man and his horse," Ross continued.

"I think I've heard this one," I said without thinking.

Fans and local citizens pay their respect to Bruce Lee and his son Brandon at the Lakeview Cemetery on a daily basis.

As I looked up, Ross appeared to wilt; belatedly I realized I might have stolen his thunder so I added, "but I think I've forgotten the details..."

Immediately, he perked up and straightened into his storytelling stance. "Well, when the graveyard was being resettled after bodies kept being shifted around, there was a man who dearly loved his horse. The man owned a plot in the cemetery, but his horse died first, so the man buried his horse in the plot. Well, the wealthy citizens of the area who had strong sensibilities were offended that they would be buried in a cemetery with a horse, so they forced the man to move his horse. After much argument, the man finally agreed to move his horse, but it's believed that he really just moved the horse to a new location in the graveyard and never told anyone where it was. Since then, there have been reports of an iridescent horse wandering around the cemetery at night."

The Civil War graveyard is a small park next to Lakeview Cemetery. Another unfortunate history of having the headstones moved around repeatedly, which has led the park being arranged in a nice circular fashion with the remaining markers, but not as many headstones as there were original internments. Where are the other bodies?

"I like to tell people on the tour when they ask where the other bodies are, to go stand in that little indentation in the ground."

Ross pointed to an imperfection at the edge of the park lawn. I judged it to be roughly six feet long.

"I tell people that if they wanted to look for one of the missing bodies after the headstones were moved, these sinkholes would be the first place I'd start."

I stood next to the spot which was no deeper than an inch or two but certainly long and wide enough to be a body.

"Is this graveyard haunted?" I asked.

Princess
Angeline's
headstone.

PRINCESS ANGELINE
BORN ~ 1811   DIED ~ MAY 31, 1896
THE DAUGHTER OF CHIEF SEALTH FOR
WHOM THE CITY OF SEATTLE IS NAMED
WAS A LIFE LONG SUPPORTER OF THE
WHITE SETTLERS, SHE WAS CONVERTED
TO CHRISTIANITY AND NAMED BY
MRS. D. S. MAYNARD.

PRINCESS ANGELINE BEFRIENDED THE
PIONEERS DURING THE INDIAN ATTACK
UPON SEATTLE ON JANUARY '26, 1896.
AT HER REQUEST SHE WAS LAID TO
REST NEAR HER PROTECTOR AND FRIEND,
HENRY L. YESLER
                SEATTLE HISTORICAL SOCIETY
                        1958

"There have been sightings of a Confederate soldier wandering the park at dusk. He's fully dressed in his gray uniform, and appears to be looking for something or someone."

Ross tapped his walking stick against his shoe and headed toward the street. I lingered for a moment, wondering just how many bodies had been separated from their grave markers.

The walk back to the Harvard Exit Theatre brought us closer to evening. It had been a very warm day, and I knew my feet would be covered in blisters. Capitol Hill as I saw it on foot and with the backdrop of hauntings, gave me a fresh burst of energy to keep searching.

Seattle's Underground

The day I went to Bill Speidel's Underground Tour, it was overcast and I packed a sweatshirt believing it would be chilly below the city. Parking in a lot just across the street on First, I barely made it to the one o'clock tour. I'd imagined a small and intimate group, but was surprised to see seventy or more people in the main room listening to a comical and sarcastic rendition of Seattle's history. Doc Maynard's Public House, the starting point for the tour, had an old-school feel to the décor as a restored 1890s building, with dark polished woods, brass accents, and burgundy drapes.

I squeezed into the back where I managed to catch the last of the introduction to Seattle's colorful and almost ridiculously farcical early endeavors to become a metropolitan city. At least the current locals have a sense of humor about the misadventures of things such as landfills of sawdust that turn into sinkholes and drown people, and an early sewer system that threatened to inundate restroom occupants if the flush chain was pulled during high tide. The host, an attractive man in his early thirties, with enough presentation and charisma in his telling to prove he'd done this introduction more than a few times, made me right at home, drawing me in to the story of Seattle as though I'd never heard it before. "So then the paper started printing the tide charts so people could get up in the morning and plan their day accordingly."

When the tales of early political corruption and sewer malfunctions drew to a close, the audience was divided into four groups and led outside where we met our guides. I lingered, waiting for the last group, and then edged toward the back to bring up the rear for pictures. We gathered on the sidewalk outside the tour office and waited for the other groups to get a head start. Meanwhile, our guide Alan launched into an explanation of the architecture.

Doc Maynard's Public House with what appears to be orb activity in the picture.

"This architectural style is called post-fire. Because, well, it came after the fire of 1889." While I found the information fascinating, I couldn't help but think ahead to the tour and hope silently, that I would get to see a ghost.

"The outer walls are the supporting walls. The interiors, where you see beams and struts, are really just to hold the floorboards up. So the true strength of these buildings rests in the stone exteriors."

Occasionally, he'd stop talking as a city bus roared by or a plane passed overhead, but I liked his presentation. Friendly and unassuming he carried the material as though it were still fresh and fascinating.

The tour in front moved far enough ahead to give us room to move in. We crossed the plaza and the crooked bend in First. As we walked, he explained the bend in First Street was because the two landowners couldn't agree on a city plan for how the streets should network. They agreed to disagree, and the city eventually bought a tiny spot between the two parcels at an elevated rate of $250,000 to connect the two halves of the town.

I guess this also accounts for the very disorienting and almost schizophrenic layout of the streets of Seattle. This I know from experience as an outsider trying to find my way around a city that has streets best described as 'counter-intuitive.'

Across the intersection and past a chocolate shop that smelled positively delicious, we came to a tiny stairway leading underground. The gate creaked and I thought, "Of course. The gate WOULD squeak."

Entrance into the Underground.

Bringing up the rear, I closed the gate behind myself and entered the darkness of underground Seattle.

Immediately, I was hit with the smell of antiquity. Heat and moisture combined with old planking, bricks, and darkness to make a unique scent of mildewed history. The Seattle underground is actually a network of sublevel corridors where the actual level of the city once resided.

After the fire of 1889, the city put an ordinance into effect that all buildings henceforth would be built fire resistant. Essentially, the new Seattle was built out of stone, and because the sea level was so close, the best way to do this meant building the city up. This was also very important for sanitation, as the early wooden pipes for sewer removal drained directly into Elliott Bay, where the tide would wash raw sewage back into the homes of citizens. Waste removal reached a technological height with the advance of the toilet and the hype of Thomas Crapper. This meant that having the city elevated could also provide a better foundation for running utilities below the city, namely the sewer.

Starting with the streets, the construction began with parallel walls along the existing sidewalks. The walls were then filled in and paved over elevating the streets from mud and tides. These raised streets could be as high as twelve feet and required the use of a ladder or steps to reach the actual street. As the buildings were constructed, the once ground level, became the basement and the street level became the new first floor.

The ground level sidewalks were only accessible at major intersections and the cumbersome ladders were often dangerous especially for women in skirts, or intoxicated pedestrians. 'Unintentional suicides' were not uncommon. Eventually, the sidewalks were also elevated to street and storefront level. Shopping continued in the basement levels for several years, necessitating the installation of glass panels into the sidewalks above for light, but as time and economy shifted, the underground became synonymous with seedy and the glass panels were replaced with thick lenses to protect the anonymity of women's undergarments from the men below. However, the life of the underground had outlived its usefulness, and as the new century gained momentum, basement shops were closed, and the former spaces put to use as storage or forgotten.

Skylights of Seattle's Underground looking out.

The Underground, as we know it today, has been obtained with special permits and the addition of railings and lights. My first impression of the underground came from the smell and the lack of circulating fresh air. Logically, I knew I wasn't breathing the same air as the people who walked the underground a hundred years ago, but it sure felt like it. Heavy and moist and not at all chilly.

I eagerly looked around for ghosts, but I saw only the backs of my tour group.

"What did they use to fill in the elevated streets?"

I didn't see who asked the question but I was certainly interested.

"Good question. There was an abundance of sawdust from the mill, but the fire proved using sawdust fill could be a potential problem. While

I'm sure they still used some, most of the fill was rubble from the fire, odd stones and bits of unusable debris. I'm sure if the cart horse died, they probably threw him in too."

While the crowd didn't seem to have a sense of humor, I at least, found the possibility of the streets of Seattle being filled with such archeological tidbits fascinating. What stories must lay hidden in the masonry of Victorian Seattle! Suddenly, the possibility of seeing a ghost was even more plausible. With such raw beginnings, in a town built right on the water—how could there not be ghosts?

At the first interesting intersection of the underground, I paid particular attention, as it was one of the only spots on the tour with a documented ghost sighting. The bank vault and the teller's cage.

Prior to the tour I called the management office who put me in touch with a former employee of Bill Speidel's Underground tour. Midge worked as a tour guide for several years in the nineties. Her account of the sighting is both exciting and intriguing.

"It was either 1995 or 1996. I don't remember which, but I know it was in the spring. We were doing a children's tour. Just kids from a school—it was one of the "Rats and Crappers" tours. We call it that because all the kids really care about is seeing a rat, or hearing the stories about the Crappers.

That spring there was a lot of construction on the sidewalks, which means the ceiling of the underground, so we had to do some detours that year. One such detour we were near the second skylight, and the kids were looking around for rats, and I noticed someone from the corner of my eye standing near the bank teller window where there used to be an old vault.

He was in his mid-thirties with brown-wavy hair the length of his ears. He was standing on the step and had a full old-fashioned mustache and pale skin.

"He was dressed in a white band-collar shirt and the top button was undone. His sleeves were rolled up once or twice, just past the wrists but not to the elbow. He was wearing old-fashioned, dark brown trousers, made out of a heavy canvas, like workman's canvas. I don't recall if he was wearing any shoes, I was so surprised I don't even re-member if he had any feet! I blinked, looked away then looked back and he was gone.

"I thought I'd imagined it. So I tried to put it out of my mind, but I thought of him a lot and even dubbed him, "The Miner," because the bank where he was standing was used to store gold during the Gold Rush.

"Five days later, I was on another 'Rats and Crapper tour' and I saw him again. I was sort of by myself and I saw him standing in the same place. I focused my attention on him and he vanished. Right in front of me. Right as I was looking at him. Then I knew I hadn't imagined him the first time. Then I knew I wasn't crazy."

"Did you notice a change in the temperature?" I asked.

"That part of the tour is always about fifteen degrees cooler than the rest of the tour, no matter what the weather is."

The teller and bank vault area where an apparition of a miner was seen.

"Did you feel or sense any negativity? Like malevolence?"

"No. None. I knew he didn't mean any harm." She paused before adding, "I almost felt like he might need help, like he was lost or something. I wasn't afraid of him."

"Have you had any other experiences like this in your life?" I questioned.

"No. Nothing. I have a sense of humor about it. I know people think it's crazy and that's okay. I don't need to convince them of anything. It just is. But I think it's fascinating."

"So you never saw him again after that?"

"I only worked there till 2001. After the earthquake, I didn't want to be underground anymore, but I always looked for him. I thought about him a lot. I imagined that if I ever saw him, I'd ask if he needed help or something."

"So about his appearance, can you tell me what your immediate impression of him was, working class, middle class, was he the bank teller, did it look like the linen of his shirt was expensive?" I wanted her first impression because although we don't like to admit it, often an appearance generates a first impression that while it might not be correct, it is often very insightful.

"No, he wasn't upper or even middle class. He was a working man. I think that's why I called him "The Miner." I think because his sleeves were rolled up and his top button undone, he wouldn't have been a gentleman, especially with those heavy working pants, like the pants construction workers wear now, but without all the loops and things."

I had no other clues to go on save those that Midge provided. His costume, and appearance and her impression of his status, plus the time that the raised street would have been under construction where the tellers cage now sits, puts his date somewhere between 1890 and 1907. My better guess is that he's closer to 1897-1903 as the Klondike Gold Rush began on July 17, 1897 and the Underground was closed in 1907 due to the fear of diseases carried by rats.

We may never know who "The Miner" is. Why is he still visiting the vault area?

I stood outside the tellers cage. Yellowed light from the modern bulbs and what seeped in from the skylight lenses cast an eerie shadow of the cage bars, and I could imagine for a moment that I wasn't alone. The tour had moved ahead sending voices and scuffs of shoes on brick down the corridor. I set up my camera and despite my surety that I was in fact alone; I took less time focusing than I should have, and the first few digital images came out blurry. After a quiet self pep talk that I was being an idiot and a reminder that I don't really believe in ghosts, I managed a couple of better images before rushing down the hallway to catch up with the group.

The teller's cage.

As I'd lingered too far in the back, the group had gone up a set of stairs to an alley and closed the gate behind them. The only thing that kept me from a minor panic attack was the fact I could see through the mesh fence where a man stood with his back to me. I struggled with the latch causing a stir wherein Alan came to rescue me.

"I see how it is," I said as I emerged onto the upper street.

"Now she's going to give me a hard time about it, and rightly so!" said my guide who smiled apologetically.

I followed behind the group as we made off down the street to another entrance to the underground. As we filed into another stairwell leading down, Alan stayed behind to shut the door making sure I was inside.

"Are you going to set up your tripod for pictures?" he asked.

"Maybe. If I need more pictures, Penny said she'd take me through again."

"Penny would be the right one to take you then."

He made sure I wasn't left behind again, which was one part relief and one part frustration. 'If I'm going to see a ghost, I'll likely need to be alone,' I thought. Unfortunately, most of the group also made sure I wasn't left alone, as there seemed to be some concern that I'd be locked in the Underground and forgotten.

As the tour continued, the heat and the smell increased. Stagnant air and moist conditions left the old walkways to develop a distinctly moldering stickiness on the back of my tongue. Remnants of a forgotten era filled the spaces below; piles of wooden beams, broken porcelain toilets elaborately decorated with blue enamel, rusted pipes, a circular red velvet sofa and a partial wall mural.

In some places, it felt as though someone's life had simply stopped existing in one place, picked up and moved elsewhere leaving behind an unfinished story. I could envision a parlor of women in turn-of-the-century gowns sitting in a hat shop discussing the latest trends in fabric. I could almost imagine them gathered near the windows, which would have been installed near the underground walkways by stairwell access points or near the lens skylights to see the newest fashions in patterns and weaves by the last of daylight as it filtered through the corridors. Ultimately, the Underground was closed when several cases of Bubonic plague emerged, and the tunnels were no longer feasible or even necessary. Even though they were primarily sealed off, some spaces were eventually opened privately as the Opium trade, prostitution, and drifters moved in over brief spans of time before the city decided to crack down and tighten up the underground. Bill Speidel saw an interest from the public, and the rest, they say, is history.

I didn't see any rats. I didn't see or feel any ghosts of a paranormal sort. I felt only the strangeness of being in a place where lives once existed in a bustling world a hundred years before me. Maybe that's all a ghost really is. I couldn't say.

A round red sofa in a section of the underground.

Later, The Seattle Ghosts Hunters put me in touch with Sheri. Sheri is affiliated with the group and eagerly told me about her experience in the Underground.

"I didn't see any ghosts while we were down there, but there was a spot where I felt like I was being watched or followed. The next morning when I was watching my husband get ready for work, I was still in bed and suddenly my body went cold and I couldn't move. I was frozen. I couldn't scream. I struggled to say my husband's name. After several attempts, I said his name and the feeling vanished. It happened three days in a row. I asked a Wiccan friend about it and she gave me some things to do and they worked. I haven't had the problem since."

"Did you feel like you were in danger?" I asked.

"Oh, absolutely. It meant me harm."

"So it was malevolent?"

"Very malevolent."

"Did you get any impression as to the life form of this malevolent being?"

Seattle's Underground walkway.

"Male. Definitely male in his thirties and he'd met with some violent end in the Underground."

"Do these sorts of things happen to you often?" I wondered.

"Actually, yes. My Wiccan friend says I have a bright spirit and that attracts these things."

"I'm just curious. How do you then protect yourself?"

"Well, she gave me some chants, and a candle for the window, and some other things in the case of the Underground ghost followed me home. She told me to have sex with my husband since the ghost seemed to be afraid of my husband. We had to do that for a week."

"Bummer," I said. "Doctor's orders…"

While I was a little let down that I didn't have a personal encounter, the tour itself was a valuable tool to glimpse the interest in Seattle's history. Not only was our tour packed, it was packed with people who were genuinely interested in the facts of the city's early beginnings. As I mentioned to several of my fellows along the tour, usually those that straggled behind the group to ensure I wasn't left, that I was writing a book on ghosts; the first thing they would ask in hushed tones with mischievous sparkling eyes was, "Have you ever seen a ghost?"

If I was disheartened about not meeting a spirit, I was at least thrilled with the level of interest from complete strangers.

A vignette view in an old shop under the city.

Steamer trunks and kegs decorate the Underground along with other miscellaneous rubble.

The old underground meat market is believed to be where the rats carrying bubonic plague originated.

The Wah Mee Massacre

The Wah Mee Massacre took place in the International District on February 18, 1983. The Wah Mee was a Chinese high-stakes gambling joint dating back to the days of Prohibition. As a speakeasy and a safe location for the Chinese to practice traditional gambling, the local cops would look the other way (for a fee) in the interest of maintaining a comfortable working and profitable relationship with the international community. The Wah Mee had a strong community orientation; in fact, the building housing the club was purchased by a conglomerate of Chinese families with the intention of maintaining a heritage for future generations. Sadly, this intention was permanently interrupted in the late winter of 1983, when three Chinese American men, barely more than boys in their early twenties, gained entrance through the front door, Willie Mak, the leader of the group, having been a frequent visitor and trusted. Once inside, the three boys hogtied the fourteen patrons and workers, then executed thirteen at point blank range. The fourteenth man was also shot, sixty-two year old Wai Chin who survived the attack and managed to crawl to get help after the boys absconded with what is reported to be "tens of thousands of dollars."

Wai Chin was able to identify the three men. Two of the killers were apprehended within hours of the murders, the third having escaped to Canada where he lived for two years before being extradited.

The Wah Mee was padlocked and left to steep in a very deep sense of grief and a strong Chinese belief in the curse of such locations where traumatic murders have occurred. I confess I know very little about traditional Chinese beliefs concerning ghosts, but one thing is certain; Maynard Alley, where the entrance to the Wah Mee club is cloaked between redbrick buildings and sloped paving . . . there sits an entrance that is by my estimation . . . creepy. The first time I stood in front of the glass bricks where the night doorman would check to see who you were before being allowed entrance, I felt eerily as though I was being watched. I chalked it up to the expectant gazes of my fellow tourists. Jake continued to tell us about the Chinese protocol involving a building owned by a group of people when such trauma occurs.

"Although the massacre took place nearly twenty-three years ago, the families owning the building have refused to rent out the space, or sell the building, or tear it down." Jake motioned to the vacant windows directly above the entrance, "It could be leased for apartments, but the families feel that, according to their tradition, the building has been cursed, and to let others enter would be to spread the curse. Therefore, they've closed the building and the padlock from the crime scene twenty-three years ago, is the same padlock that is on the door today. In fact, no one has been in the building since."

Jake encouraged us all to look inside the small glass brick peephole. I stepped up to the window and stood on my toes. Waiting for my eyes to adjust to the darkness inside, I felt a little ridiculous. What was I expecting to see? Ghosts in the flesh?

It was worse, in a sense… the guard position of the entrance was a mess of disarray that showed the signs of the night that had taken thirteen lives and left a community in shocked grief. A delicate porcelain tea cup was overturned on the counter, odds and ends strewn about, a heavy layer of dust and a network of cobwebs made the glimpse into history feel a lot like a cross between a dime show walk-through at a Halloween house, and a surreal window into another world where bad people do horrible things leaving the world to survive the repercussions of their greed.

"The room has been left exactly the way it was after the massacre. Nothing has been touched. No one is allowed entry, but this little window is left for us to see what remains."

I shuddered and stepped back so the next person on the tour could look. It was getting colder outside, but I didn't think for a moment that the chill was only the air—the place didn't sit well around me. After taking a few pictures, I loitered near the opposite building in an attempt not to look like I was trying to get away.

"I have a few pictures here. I want everyone to be able to take a look before I tell you about them." Jake passed around two 8 x 10s and I took my time looking at what appeared to be the exact view of the entrance that we all stood in front of. I hoped to see something.

"Do you see anything unusual?" Jake asked.

"I can't tell if it's the light or the picture, but it looks like this glass brick is different in the photo than in real life?" I studied the picture and realized I was TRYING to make something out of nothing. I shrugged and passed the pictures down the line.

Entrance to the
Wah Mee.

A glimpse inside the peep-hole.

When everyone had sufficiently studied the photos, Jake explained, "On one of these very tours a woman took this picture of the entrance and captured this picture of a face looking out the peephole. That clear glass brick that you all just looked inside. I was here when she took it, and I can say I've seen the same face looking out of the glass from the corner of my eye."

The pictures came around again and I stared, crossed my eyes, squinted and held the picture closer to my face but I couldn't for the life of me, see the ghost looking out the peephole. Others nodded and exclaimed how they didn't notice it before. I felt a little foolish, but I really couldn't see it.

"Can you see it?" Jake asked me.

"No, not really. I still think that brick looks different, but I don't see a face or a ghost." However silly it sounds to say it, I felt terribly letdown. I was on the tour to gather stories, find ghosts, explore the haunted phenomenon—and I couldn't even see the face everyone else made out plain as day.

"That's okay." Jake patted my shoulder and nodded compassionately.

I would take Jake's tour again, several months later to refresh my research. The second time, I stood outside the Wah Mee, I felt queasy and while it could have been the time of evening, just before sunset, I developed a fierce case of the chills. I wondered if I were coming down with the flu. Again, I looked inside and again felt a sad sense of loss for people I'd never met. I stepped back and let Jake continue with the pictures. Again, I strained my eyes looking for a face—hoping that I would be able to make out a shadow or an eye, but I still couldn't see it. It seemed like a throwback to grade school when the teacher puts an abstract set of lines on the chalkboard and asks you if you see the old lady walking the dog. You WANT to see it. You HOPE to see it. Ultimately when one person claims to see it, others follow. But then there's me. Despite my best attempts, I simply couldn't see the face.

My shivering got perpetually worse and eventually a woman on the tour loaned me her sweater. Later that evening, as the tour ended, I was supposed to sit down with Jake and AJ to talk shop and the paranormal, but I was so sick by the time the tour ended, that I quickly bolted for home where I spent the next two days in bed with soup.

Several people asked me if I'd been sick prior to the tour or if it suddenly developed while visiting haunted locations. I had, in fact, been tired and achy for a couple days before the tour. I'd attributed it to stress and the anxiety of meeting a deadline, but I also freely admit the fact that during the three hours in the van for my second go around with Jake and Private Eye Tours, my body's flu like symptoms escalated faster than I thought possible. The fierceness of the chills alone alarmed me; the nausea also gave me a bit of a start.

On the advice of a friend and spiritual practitioner who asked me to "humor her," I practiced a protective meditation, burned sage in my room, and spritzed myself with sage-infused water. I also lit a candle and placed it in the window. For the next couple of days I treated myself as though I'd picked up the latest flu bug and thought nothing of it till much later when I heard quite by accident, that brushing up against a spirit that sticks to your energy field can make you ill.

Still not entirely convinced of ghosts as they are portrayed, I shrugged it off. That doesn't, however, negate the fact that I was very uneasy around the building where the infamous Wah Mee massacre took place. I have no intention of ever returning to that location.

Short Legends

The Burnley School of Art

The story of Burnley, as the ghost has been named, has many variations. The most repeated details claim that a young man who was a student at the school was either shoved or fell down the stairs, but the end result is that he died in the school.

Burnley is considered a very rowdy ghost and I heard it said on one occasion, "Well, he's a boy! What do you expect?"

What indeed? Burnley has been blamed for doors opening and closing, footsteps, the coffee pot being turned on when no one else was around, phones dialing themselves, furniture being rearranged, papers being wadded up, lights flickering, and desks drawers being spontaneously opened.

One account of the security system claims that the building owners got so fed up with the alarm tripping and the guards showing up to a false alarm, which the owners still had to pay for, that the owner gave the keys and security over to the daughter who repeated with exasperation that she never got any sleep for running to shut the alarm off every night.

Burnley is also held to blame for an incident that involved a pretty young woman on the top floor. As she was looking out the window, she claims that someone shoved her with powerful and malicious intent toward the window. She spun about, but remained the only person in the room. Since then, there have been complaints of women being pinched, having their hair pulled, and unseen hands "groping" them.

There was also a report from a night janitor that he cleaned a room, went into the hall, and shut the door behind himself, whereupon he heard a tremendous crash and quickly reentered the room to discover the desks had been overturned and stacked in a pile.

Burnley School of Art.

There have been stories of séances and mediums who have attempted to discover what Burnley wants and who he was. One medium is positive that Burnley was an eighteen-year-old boy who died in 1913 after a school basketball game.

Whoever Burnley was, it seems fairly evident that he's in no hurry to move on. It's my opinion that he likes having the school as his personal playground and will continue to haunt the location so long as there are pretty girls to pester and non-believers to surprise.

Amazon Building

There is a distinctive building in Seattle that once served as the VA Hospital. An orange-red art deco building that sits on Beacon Hill at the juncture of I-5 and I-90 E. Currently Amazon.com calls this masterful piece of architecture home, but so do several spirits. The space is reported to have a nurse in residence that wafts a specific brand of perfume through the lobby and first floor. Many people claim to smell something "beautiful," perhaps a combination of gardenia and orange blossoms and something else indefinable. Other unexplained phenomena involves a hospital gurney, or at least the sound of a gurney with a wheel that needs oil. Several people have mentioned hearing the gurney behind them only to turn and realize they are alone in the hall. Bathroom faucets are said to turn on and off, and occasionally lights flicker.

The Golf Course

There is a story often repeated about a naked Indian on the golf course. Apparently, in the 1950s and 1960s, there were several sightings of an Indian dancing around in a circle while chanting. Modest viewers were outraged by the dancer's nudity and would call the police, others called because the Indian was interfering with their game. Whoever the storyteller was, the ending was always the same. Police would converge on the golf course and surround the naked man so he had no way of escape. Then the officers rush, and as they close in, the naked Indian vanishes into thin air, leaving behind a muddle of confused onlookers.

Highway 101

A legend exists, perhaps to scare young women from driving alone at night on Highway 101. It's said that a bandaged and bloody man wanders the side of the highway late at night. The story claims that during the early days of Seattle, when logging was in full swing—a logger was crushed by a falling tree. His fellows bandaged him up the best they could and put him in the back of a carriage bound for the hospital in town. Stories differ as to whether he fell off the carriage in route or simply died during transport, but the end is the same… now the bloody bandaged logger wanders Highway 101 at night.

Pier 70

There is a persistent story about a good ghost that I've heard several times from different sources and I can honestly say . . . it is unique. The story goes on that when people are in the pits of despair; on the verge of suicide or feeling defeated, they often find themselves standing on Pier 70. Some accounts claim individuals show up at the pier with the conscious intent of leaping off. To their surprise, a fog bank or mist or even a shadowy trick of light approaches the pier, and out of this mirage emerges a clipper ship. The ghostly clipper ship and her captain appear plain as day to the person in despair, but others on the pier claim to see nothing. Not that it matters, because the captain is there only for the person in trouble. He speaks to the struggling individual, encouraging them not to give up. By all accounts, he gives the equivalent of a pep talk that all their fortunes will improve so long as they hang in there.

Be it a true story or not, I personally love the idea of a ghostly pep talk, and the romantic ending given at the end of each story is that—yes indeed, their fortunes improve. Now, that's the kind of ghost story I'd like to encounter first hand!

The Moore Theatre

The theatre is located in Downtown Seattle and is said to be the home of at least one spirit. Legend says that in the 1980s, an employee called in a psychic and several others to conduct a séance and communicate with the ghost in hopes of discovering what it wanted. Stories claim that the night manager burst in and caught the group around a table and fired the employee on the spot before chasing the others out of the building. Since then, the night manager is supposedly haunted by heavy breathing on the back of his neck wherever he goes. Another story I was unable to verify, but its fun none the less and a fantastic fright tale to encourage night managers to be kind to their employees.

The Neptune Theatre

Located on 45th very near the University of Washington campus, the Neptune is another one of Seattle's Theatre's to suffer the continued visits of a portly man often seen smoking. But more often, he's noticed as the smell of tobacco. He's said to pick on girls by pinching their shoulders or backsides or even tweaking their hair.

The Neptune Theatre on 45th.

Hotel Andra

Formerly know as the Claremont Hotel established in the mid 1920s, Hotel Andra has reported sounds of jazz on the 9th floor. During the days of Prohibition, it's said that Hotel Andra hosted parties for the elite who would drink and dance while the local authorities looked the other way due to the high class of the citizens. There is one reported death when a worker fell to her death in the 1960s from an upper floor. However, the noises and thumping from the 9th floor, which have been repeatedly brought to the attention of the staff by guests, seem to be of a more jovial and happy nature than a tragic accidental death. Perhaps, the ghosts of Hotel Andra are simply reliving the best days of their lives.

Suzzalo Library

AJ delighted in telling me a story of the winter rain ghost at the Suzzalo Library. The library is located on the University of Washington campus and towers over the landscape with breathtaking architecture that reminded me of something Gothic fairly oozing history with its spires. I felt a flutter in my belly that I couldn't explain upon entering the building for the first time. Masonic symbols and stained glass windows, marble floors, and solid oak railings, combined with the oppressive silence of a place of leaning and the heavy scent of books gave me a full-body shudder. I felt perfectly at home.

The story claims that a girl in a 1960s outfit and rain goulashes appears at the library during the rainy winter months and disappears up the marble spiral staircase. She only appears when it's raining, and she never leaves wet footprints or drips on the floor. When the library closes at night she can never be found.

The Suzzalo Library is visited by a phantom girl on rainy days.

Green Lake

I first heard this story from AJ and Joe from Seattle Ghost Hunters. They asked if I'd heard of the apparitions at Green Lake, and when I said I hadn't, they both exclaimed in surprise and talked over one another to spill the gory details.

The reports have claimed seeing the body of a naked woman, battered and beaten, lying dead in the grass near the water's edge. Other accounts are of a wandering woman in white, or a woman weeping. When the police are called or the women are approached, the apparitions vanish.

It's believed that this manifestation is actually the ghost of Sylvia Gaines whose naked body was discovered murdered on June 17, 1926. Gaines Point at the northern end of Green Lake was named in her honor.

Bob Gaines, Sylvia's own father, was arrested and found guilty of her murder which was a headliner case of incest, jealousy, and murderous rage. Sylvia was twenty-two years old and is said to resemble the ghostly woman who appears in multiple stages of grief and death.

Daughters of the American Revolution

The D.A.R building is located diagonally across the street from the Harvard Exit Theatre. The Daughters of the American Revolution rent the space out for special occasions even though there are multiple reports of flickering lights, voices, and old music. There are two accounts of women in

The D. A. R. Building.

late 1800s-style dress either walking down the front stairs or pacing in the front room. The very nearness of this building to the Harvard Exit is interesting, considering the Harvard Exit Theatre is such a paranormal hotspot.

Hugo House

The Richard Hugo House is located on Capitol Hill and is currently a center for encouraging the written word. Writers and teachers are in residence at the former home of the famous poet. When I spoke with Darren from WSPIR (Washington State Paranormal Investigations and Research), he explained that they had gone to investigate the home after several accounts of unusual occurrences had taken place, including the apparition of a young girl in the basement who appeared only from the waist up. Aside from minor EMF activity there was little to report. Darren explained that the building was once a mortuary.

I couldn't find any other reports of the Hugo House, except for the frequent confirmations of, "The Hugo House is haunted." But when I questioned further, no one had any other stories to tell.

These short stories and legends are so frequently repeated, that the variations are as tangled as I think they can possibly get. This only adds to the fun of collecting them. Whether the apparitions are tall or short, missing hands or missing feet the story is still entertaining. Tracking down the truth of such encounters is an impossibility. The only fact inherent in these tales that is verifiable is the fact that no matter where I went, who I talked to about these locations—everyone enjoyed the telling.

Pike Place Market

Established in 1907, Seattle's first public market was an immediate success. Due to price gouging and general corruption of middle-merchants, the public market required that only the producer of a product could sell to the buyer. This fueled the agricultural and economic burst of the new century.

The "market" began as a row of wagons lined up each morning to sell their wares. This grew to a line of covered stalls and eventually a city within the city of Seattle. Its current multi-leveled warren of shops, stalls, and cafés is due to the rescue and renovation efforts of the 1970s, and to this day, is a foundation for tourism and the promotion of agriculture, arts, and crafts. With an establishment that maintains a heavy population both residential and visitor, it's fairly reasonable to expect that in the ninety-nine years the market has operated, there would be a bevy of great ghost stories.

On the western end of downtown Seattle, the Market is not only very near the water, it is also reportedly constructed on land that had once been a native trade ground for multiple tribes, as well as a convergence of ley lines.

The sculpture created by Michael Orin called, *The Point,* is said to have been made to honor this tradition. Located in the back of the market, *The Point* is a triangular piece of sandstone with geometric and spiral etchings in various levels. This piece of art is said to be resting on the spot where three major ley lines come together, and those who meditate near it will be able to see a shimmer just above the sculpture.

The most notable ghost in this area is also the daughter of Seattle's namesake, Princess Angeline. Chief Seattle's daughter lived near the water in a shack and came to the market for decades. While most natives were being pushed on to reservations or being forcibly removed from city limits, Princess Angeline continued to be a much-loved resident of the downtown area. Princess Angeline was as much an icon as her late father, and was held in regard by Henry Yesler, one of Seattle's founding patrons. When Angeline died on May 31, 1896, she was in her late seventies and per her last request, she was buried in Lake View Cemetery near her friend Yesler. Over the years, her ghost has been spotted walking through the market or wandering the grounds near where her shack once stood, which occupied land on Western Avenue between Pine and Pike streets.

She's been reported to be weaving baskets, which she did when she was alive, and carrying laundry or counting beads. Stories also claim she glows incandescent blue or white. She's easily recognizable to Seattle residents who are familiar with her legacy. She is an old woman walking with a hunch; her wrinkled face and characteristic headscarf always tied in a knot under the chin would be more than enough identification, but even people who don't know about her history and her famous blue eyes, have remarked that it's unusual to see a native with blue eyes. When they're told it was in fact a specter, few can believe it, but locals of the market know there isn't any other figure with that description and eyes like the sea.

The Point, by Michael Orin.

At some point in the last hundred years, Princess Angeline's spirit has been tarred with the myth of the curse. The curse claims that if you happen to be unlucky enough to see Princess Angeline, you will die shortly thereafter. I have yet to find evidence of this claim. In fact, there seems to be far more sightings by people who are happy to talk about it. The impression passed along is that they feel blessed for being given a chance to be a witness.

Although, one of my favorite stories given to me by AJ Downey goes something like this…at a wedding downtown the bride and groom were exchanging vows when an unknown woman appeared in the party. The father of the bride became angry and confrontational to the woman, shouting "Who let this homeless bag lady in here?" As men drew closer to "escort" her out she vanished right before them all.

After hearing the story, I immediately asked, "Oh my god! Did anyone die?"

AJ snorted and looked at me as though I were idiot. "No. That's just a myth."

Upon my arrival to Seattle, Pike's Market and the Space Needle were the two touristy things I'd scheduled to do just for myself. I thought it would take me a couple of hours to wander through the market, snap a few photos, have a coffee, and so on. I'm now convinced that only a month of solid Sundays could show me all the nooks and crannies and adorable cubby holes full of treasure. Day after day I went to the market shouldering my way through the throngs of tourists and locals alike. The sound is nearly deafening, the smells are a cacophony of fish, people, espresso, candy, flowers, and fresh pastries.

I'd walk down, grab an Americano and just watch the people. Haunted or not, there's one thing that is plain for anyone to see—there is a spirit in the market. A spirit that was born ninety-nine years ago and lives today in the partnership of farmers and their buyers. The community essence is so powerful in the west corner of the city, you can almost feel the idea of global co-operation, love of humanity, encouragement of the arts, and the spirit of brotherhood as though it were an actual living breathing being hovering over the area. I believe this explains why in my research of the ghost stories in the market there are many entities and few malicious energies.

Before Pike Place opens, it feels like a ghost town.

For example, one ghost is reportedly the lingering phantasm of the Market Manager, Arthur Goodwin, who is best known for his improvements to the lighting and aesthetics of the flower boxes and free vaudeville shows. Evidently he was a fantastic promoter and the Market did well under his early days.

The ghost in the Goodwin Library is said to be him, as his offices were up above the market. It's claimed that he often stands at the window in bad weather to watch the goings on.

Another ghost exists in the folklore of the market as a Swing Dancer. Stories claim that as women got off shift in WWII working at the Boeing plant, they'd come to the Market where a dance hall had been set up. Women were said to have danced with a handsome young gentleman who by all accounts was an excellent dancer. Although he was mannerly and courteous, he often disappeared into thin air before witnesses and disappointed women without so much as a polite "good bye."

Many of these stories are impossible to corroborate with witnesses because of their age and the frequency by which they are passed by word of mouth and changed in the retelling. Whether there is truth in these accounts—even a grain—I'll probably never know. The point of interest for me is not so much in the truth and minutia of each sighting, but the belief of those who tell the stories.

The Market populace believes these stories to be as much an integral part of the history and the energy of the experience as the grocers, craftsmen, and the tourists. I think it's fair to say that they are proud of their specters and live harmoniously and with open minds.

Proof of this exists in the enthusiasm of the haunted tours and booklets provided. I signed up for the Market Ghost Tours with Mercedes Yaeger who came highly recommended by Jake and the Seattle Ghost Hunters.

Mercedes practically grew up in the Market and her father, Michael, has written a great deal in regards to the Market history and the ghostly residents. So it's with a solid family tradition that Mercedes took me and a handful of others on a walking tour to visit all the haunted locations of the Market—which makes up roughly four blocks of multi-leveled commerce.

The other members of my tour consisted of a couple from Boston, who'd taken the Underground tour with Mercedes as a guide, a family of four from Chicago, and a young writer for a local magazine who was working on the upcoming Halloween article.

Mercedes wore a bowler hat with a business card tucked into the strap in the front. While I thought it was cute, I didn't understand until we started moving that it wasn't simply an adorable gimmick—it served as a marker so we could see her as we moved through the crowd.

Mercedes is a born show woman and as we followed her past fish-mongers who catered to the tourists by throwing fish and posing for pictures with large clams, she started telling us about the history of the renovation and Friends of the Market who banded together to keep the area from being demolished in the 1960s.

Impossible to believe it, but at one time there had been a push to tear down the Market and build parking and offices for the view. On the tour we passed nearly every nationality, shape, size, and age of persons. We walked past vendors and street performers and fruit so fresh and ripe you could smell the peaches three stalls over. How could anyone think of tearing down the Market?

"That window up there." Mercedes pointed to a spot on the wall above the landing. "That used to be the LaSalle. A bordello."

"What's that?" asked one of the younger girls from Chicago.

Mercedes looked at the mother, "Uhm… does she know what a brothel is?"

The girl, perhaps twelve, shot back, "Of course I know what a brothel is."

"Oh, okay… well, a bordello is the same thing."

The LaSalle Hotel was run by Nellie Curtis, who'd acquired the hotel from a Japanese family forced to sell below the value as they were pushed into an internment camp during WWII. Nellie managed to run the hotel as a legitimate business, but still maintained her reputation as a Madame housing "ladies of ill repute." When the fleet would dock, her ladies would hand out cards that said, "LaSalle Hotel, friends easily made." By all accounts, sailors lined up to make easy friends.

"See that balcony?" Mercedes pointed to the area near the window. "That used to lead to stairs that went all the way to the waterfront. Girls used to sit out there to attract men. They would sit under the glow of the red light."

Over the years there have been claims of women sitting in thin air, brushing their hair or lounging where there once there were stairs.

The stairs of LaSalle Hotel have been replaced by trees.

We moved on to where a wooden ramp led down to the bottom level. "This ramp is the original wood put in when the market was first built. Can you imagine how many millions of people have walked up or down this ramp?"

Indeed the wood was worn to a shiny polish in places and the knots stood out in relief. We waited for people to pass, before moving on. "This is were the stables were. Farmers would bring their wagons and horses here, and children would help load and unload the carts as well as take care of the horses."

The original ramp has been worn smooth by ninety-nine years of tread.

Down the ramp, we stopped in front of Grandma's Attic—a trinket shop full of figurines and small toys. Bonnie has owned and managed the shop for thirty-seven years. When I asked her if she'd ever felt uncomfortable or threatened she gave a hearty, "Oh, No. Absolutely not. Our ghosts are friendly ghosts."

Bonnie's experience goes something like this, "One day I came in and two display cases on opposite sides of the room had been cracked. The door was still locked when I got there, and nothing was missing, but the display case showed the doll house furniture was closed and the furniture from the third shelf was on the second shelf and all piled up."

There were no other reports of cracked glass on the floor, no earthquakes or reported break-ins. There appears to be no explanation for the event. Bonnie claims nothing like it had happened before or since, and that her interpretation is that the ghosts were in the toys shop having a party.

"Do you know of other instances in the market?" I wondered.

"Have you heard of the "bookstore ghost?" There's a bookstore down the hall from me called Shakespeare & Co. Books. The woman who owned it was smart and intelligent. She used to come to work in the morning, and there was a book that would fall off the shelf and open to a specific spot every day. She would always put the book back and it would happen the next day."

And then there's Jacob who lives in the bead shop. Now currently The Bead Zone, located down under on the 4th floor. Jacob, as the spirit

Bonnie has owned and operated Grandma's Attic for thirty-seven years.

has been named, is a playful and mischievous presence that has been with the owners since they opened in 2001. Jacob is believed to be one of the children that worked in the market as a stable boy or a grocer's helper. The Bead Zone is actually very near where the stables once stood. The lore of The Bead Zone claims that when new owners bought the place, they knocked down a wall, and inside a nook in the wall was a collection of beads and pennies and small toys. Legend has it that there was a penny for every year for the last eighty years all the way up to the year the nook was discovered—even though the wall was sealed.

I spoke with Ram, who owns The Bead Zone with his wife Nina. Ram spoke about the spirit nonchalantly, and with a great deal of affection. The interior of the store is brightly lit and full of colorful beads, stones, and threads. According to Ram, the spirit of Jacob is playful and mischievous. At the end of the day, the shop workers will sort the beads into separate containers on the tables always keeping the shades and colors apart. When the shop is opened in the morning, the beads are shuffled and in mixed containers.

Ram also told me that once when his wife was on the phone, and became agitated as loops of beads flew off the wall across the room. Nina spoke to Jacob's spirit in a firm but kind tone saying, "Stop." The activity stopped at once.

The day I went in to visit the shop for the interview, Ram showed me a camera that had been set up by a local paranormal research group. He explained that there was a great deal of interest in the shop's ghost, and several people had come to investigate.

October 3, 1918, brought the Spanish Influenza to Seattle. The Influenza was responsible world-wide deaths for nearly twenty-one million people. Within six months of the Influenza's arrival in Seattle 1,600 people died of Pulmonary Edema (fluid in the lungs). (Some sources claim that it could have killed as many as 100 million people worldwide.)

Many shop owners who have lived with the ghosts near the stables, believe they are the spirits of children—perhaps children from the days of the pandemic or even earlier when orphans lived in the stalls with the horses and carried baskets for shoppers.

This might explain the disturbances in Grandma's Attic as well as The Bead Zone, as both of these locations are very brightly lit, colorful, and imbued with a jovial and youthful energy. It's possible, in my estimation, that these two environments would be attractive for children, especially orphans who may have had little or no childlike experiences.

The tour took us out to the stairs leading to Western Avenue, where *The Point* sits in an alcove. Down the street and up another set of stairs we came to a section of the Market where the tiles laid in the floor were inscribed with the names of those who contributed funds to the reconstruction.

There's something distinctly weird about stepping on hundreds of names, especially when one of the tiles was purchased by The Heaven's Gate UFO cult. The group committed mass suicide in 1997 when the comet Hale-Bopp passed over. Whether I believe in ghosts or not, I gave that tile a wide berth.

Mercedes walked us up through the busy streets to the northern end of the Market and Post Alley where she talked about Seattle's first mortuary, which I'll discuss later in its own chapter, ER Butterworth & Sons.

When the group dispersed, I sat down to chat with Mercedes and discovered that the paranormal interests of Seattleites is fairly open-minded and would venture toward curious. She was quick to point me in the direction of the other Market Ghost tour offered by Sheila Lyon.

Sheila owns the Market Magic and Novelty shop. Conducting tours from her shop and avidly researching the histories behind the hauntings, Sheila generously offered to take me on a private tour. I was struck by how at home she seemed at the Market, and I followed her dark curly head through the crowd to the "Haunted Column."

"They say this column is haunted, because it's always cooler in this space by several degrees. Once they brought a ghost hunting team up with equipment and the readings started to go nuts right in this spot. Can you feel it? Here step up, then step back."

I dutifully stepped in and out of the area around the column. I didn't feel any significant difference. "Is there any history surrounding this pillar?" I asked.

"No. Not that I could find. It's just interesting." She shrugged. "And that shop up there, is a barber shop. There are a lot of reports about people hearing the "Fat Lady Barber" singing at night."

"I've heard of the Lady Barber."

"Have you heard that she used to lull men into the shop with songs? She'd massage their faces and trim their hair and give them a shave—all while singing until they feel asleep. Then when they were comfortably snoozing she'd pick their pockets."

"Yes. I'd heard that. I'd also heard that her ghost was from the renovation and that she fell through the floorboards and died. However, I was never able to verify this. I couldn't find any record of a woman falling through the floor."

She waived a hand dismissively, and rolled her eyes. "I never found that either. But I can tell you that the night janitors report hearing her sing quite regularly." She laughed. "One janitor told me whenever he hears her music he checks his pockets."

The crowd thinned out and I moved toward the center of the hallway to get a better view of the stores.

"I was hoping you might explain why there are so many toy shops in this area that have events, and by all accounts do fairly well."

"Well, this bag store here, right down the way from the Bead Zone, used to be a marionette store. They used to open the shop in the morning and discover that their locked store had been played in. All the puppets would be moved around and the strings tangled."

"Is that why they moved?" I wondered.

"I don't think so. They're still in Seattle. I think they just needed a bigger store."

"Have you heard any other accounts in the Market?"

"There used to be a store downstairs, run by a fortune teller named Madame Nora who used a technique called Egyptian sand divination. After she died, the shop was leased to an Egyptian family who claims that one day a hunched old woman in a scarf came in with a crystal ball. She set the ball on the counter, picked up a scarab statue about the size of a hand and walked away, without so much as a word." She led me down the stairs toward the Egyptian import store. "They say the crystal ball she left is haunted. But it isn't, I bought it and it's not haunted."

We stopped outside the import store, where she explained the interior used to have a replica of the pyramid where the scarabs were place around it on the floor.

"They think the woman who came in was Madam Nora—or her ghost anyway."

As we made our way back up the stairs to the magic shop, I said, "I seem to be having trouble with the accounts of the Indian woman with the young boy, and Princess Angeline. I find them as distinct and separate stories, but many of the sources I've come across clump them together. Are there two stories, or is Princess Angeline seen with a little boy sometimes?"

"They are separate. Accounts of the Indian woman with the little boy describe a woman who is much younger than the reported sightings of Princess Angeline. The Indian woman and the little boy are most often seen near the Bead Zone, and the stairs in that section of the hallway. Princess Angeline is seen everywhere. In fact, it was said in the early days of the Market lore that she was a champion of the farmer. Any time one of the farmers was being cheated, Angeline would appear in silent support."

"I hadn't heard that."

"Oh and do you know about the dime-a-dance ghost?"

"I've heard of the *Swing Shift Ghost* up in the dance hall."

"When the workers would get off the swing shift at the Boeing plant?"

"Yeah, I've heard of that story, but again not sources to back it up."

"Well, I personally talked to three ladies, I guess they're in their eighties now, but they all told me about him separately—I didn't even ask about him. They would tell me about going to the dance hall, where they'd wait their turn to dance. I asked them how they'd know it was their turn, they all said, "You just knew honey, you just knew.""

I laughed. "What did he look like?"

"They all said he was "well dressed" in a double-breasted suit."

"Wow. Double breasted, that sounds more like 1920-1930. The Boeing plant war shift was the early to mid forties."

"Yes, that does sound like a 1920's."

(Later my curiosity would drive me to the internet to discover the prevalence of the double-breasted fashion. While most popular in the 1920s and 1930s, there was a version of the 1940s Zoot suit.)

"One thing they all commented on was how shiny his shoes were. One woman said it was what she remembered most, 'his shoes were shined until they gleamed.'"

"I like that story." I smiled completely charmed by the idea of a glitzy-stylish man showing up to dance with the real "Rosie the Riveters" after the swing-shift to show them all a good time, despite the fact they were probably exhausted after long days at the plant, and worried about their loved ones in the war; I'm sure they loved it, even looked forward to it. Whether the story is true or not, it's one of those tales that made me happy to be out digging up folklore.

"You should mention Mr. D's also," she said, glancing off in the direction of a group of people maneuvering through the hall toward the magic shop.

"Do you have first hand accounts of the Greek Deli?"

"I've talked to him; Mr. D's Greek Deli is across the street. Sometimes he sculpts famous faces out of meat and leaves them in the freezer. When he brings people to look at them, they're sometimes missing an ear or the tip of the nose. He says the employees don't do it. He's got kind of a humorous and laid back approach to why it happens. He says in Greece the spirits battle with one another. Like the time he sculpted Jay Leno and David Letterman and the next day they were all damaged. He say's in his country, the spirits of competing individuals will battle one another."

"Have you heard of any spots around town with interesting, unexplainable things?" I asked.

"Have you heard of the Shadow Box?"

I shook my head.

"I have a friend who was a piano player. He'd go to the Shadow Box after hours to use their piano to practice on, since he didn't have his own. So he'd be alone there from two in the morning till about four. He told me that sometimes when he'd go to the bathroom, he could hear the piano playing without him."

"Okay, that would creep me out."

She nodded. "Me too."

Overall, Pikes Place Market was my favorite place, not only for research, but for the atmosphere of Seattle. I found myself at The Market around 9 am with the intention of gathering photos or interviews, and after a cup of coffee and a fresh pastry, I would realize I'd lost two hours just wandering around the vendors. If I were a ghost in Seattle, or even in Downtown, I'd want to hang out at Pikes simply to soak in the vibrancy of the living. It could be my imagination, but the atmosphere and the bubble of enthusiasm that defines the stalls and the stores, makes the coffee taste better and the food richer, and with people like Mercedes and Sheila, you can't go wrong with company that entertains you with great stories.

Ted Bundy

The first time I went to Ted Bundy's house near the University of Washington, I still firmly sat on the fence as to whether ghosts existed or not. I didn't need to go inside to feel the creepy oiliness of something not quite right.

Ted Bundy shocked the world in the 1970s with a confessional of thirty victims. Often dismembered, strangled or bludgeoned, the women he murdered and sexually assaulted were left at dump sites. However, he did occasionally keep the heads of some of his victims in the freezer of his house. The property near the University where Ted Bundy once lived and reportedly kept the heads of at least four of his victims was vacant when I stopped by for the very first time. I was told the landlords couldn't keep it rented, and after it sat in the market for nearly a year they gave up trying to sell it.

The craftsman style home was painted white, and although it was near sunset, I could clearly see through the first floor windows to an empty room. Ted Bundy typically preyed on young women in their mid-teens to mid-twenties with long straight hair. Said to be an attractive and charismatic man, Ted Bundy often gained the trust of his victims by faking an injury or appearing helpless. As I looked at the house, I couldn't even imagine the force of brutality or the grief he left behind.

That night after the first week of my research, I went home to my friends' house where I was staying to watch their cats while I worked in Seattle. My self professed disbelief in ghosts wasn't shaken, but my sense of humanity certainly felt dented. Shivering, I crawled into bed with the two cats and watched the door to my bedroom with a sense of anxiety I couldn't explain.

Call it the lingering bad mojo of a trip to the home of one of the most notorious serial killers in recent history, or the weight of realizing

that the world is capable of turning out some seriously evil people …
but I think it's safe to sum up the experience as a brush with history that
left an oil slick on my innocence.

Ted Bundy was executed by electrocution on January 24, 1989.

Still needing to do the research, I was sure not to go back alone. While
I'm not a psychic or an intuitive, I sensed something that I could not
adequately describe with words. I felt as though things there at that house
were … unfinished. The group I returned with was part of a tour, and at
least one woman on the tour took pictures of the house with her digital
camera that showed clear and present orb activity. Others expressed a
sense of unease, and I saw another woman visibly shudder.

I simply felt depressed, oppressed. Again, I felt as though things
were without closure, and although I didn't know how to express this
sensation, I suddenly had a thought that although I was writing a book
on Ghosts of Seattle, Ted Bundy would get no more publicity from me
than a couple of pages. A footnote as it were. I refused to take pictures
of his home based on principle, and when I left with the tour the last
time, I decided after my book was published, I'd leave his nasty business
to the underbelly of time and think no more about him.

That night, I wondered why I had such a strong conviction to this
idea. Perhaps it was my imagination, but it seemed to me that he wanted
the exposure, the attention, the grandstanding … Ghost or not, that
kind of evil deserves no place in my book.

Starvation Heights

Then there's the story of Starvation Heights. No, this isn't the latest Hollywood ingénue weight trend; it's one of the more famous stories of the Pacific Northwest and one of the few documented cases of a female serial killer. Dr. Linda Burfield Hazzard was by all accounts a very dynamic and strong personality. The hauntings of the Butterworth funeral home, now known as Kell's and The Starlite Lounge, and the infamous murders of Dr. Hazzard which mostly took place in Olalla are tied by rumors and a heavy dose of theatrics.

It's not unknown that the Pacific Northwest has its share of serial killers, Ted Bundy & Gary Ridgway, the Green River killer, being the most famous. But the story of Linda Hazzard and Starvation Heights is a sadistic tale of evil and coercion on a scale that so shocked and horrified the citizens of Seattle in the early 1900s, that it has become a main staple of campfire horror and bedtime boogeyman threats.

After reading the book Starvation Heights, by Gregg Olsen, I promptly took myself out to a solo dinner of belt-popping proportions. The brilliant part of the ghostly aspect of this tale is that it preys on a primal animal fear—the need to eat, the necessity of sustenance which drives the most basic functions of our form.

Dr. Linda Burfield Hazzard is credited for the starvation deaths of thirteen people, but many suspect the true number sits somewhere between thirty to forty. In this day and age, it's difficult to imagine how anyone could put themselves in a position to be slowly starved to death while having your jewels, clothes, and even your inheritance signed over to the very person responsible for your condition. But imagine for a moment, that you are unwell— sickly even—and your very compassionate- authoritative medical practitioner regularly assures you that with her treatment you will be better than new. People trust the elevated positions of their doctors everyday. People imbue their health care providers with absolute power over their body everyday—so the position that Claire and Dora Williamson, among many others, found themselves in is not actually out of the realm of the imagination. In fact, the particular kind of hell in which they lived is so realistic that it evokes a deep sense of empathy and fear in everyone who hears the tale.

While Olalla is actually not a part of the greater Seattle area, Dr. Hazzard maintained her offices in downtown, by commuting daily on the ferry. Along with her offices in town, her initial therapy of the two most famous victims of her "treatment" were originally housed in Seattle's downtown area. For the most part, Dr. Hazzard also performed her autopsies, burials, and even cremations after the construction of her crematorium, due to the tragically high body count of her tactics; these were all taken care of in Olalla. However, for the occasion of a few funerals and viewings, like in the case of Claire Williamson, the body was shipped by boat to the funeral home of ER Butterworth & Sons.

The Williamson sisters were wealthy, and according to the book by Gregg Olsen, prone to naiveté and fad treatments. When they discovered the new book *Fasting for the Cure of Disease*, by Dr. Linda Hazzard in 1910, the sisters quickly enrolled in the diet that would claim Claire's life. It's not a simple thing to say she starved to death. That statement would only be a partial truth, because the true terror of Linda Hazzard's victims comes in her convictions that killing these people was the right thing to do. In her mind, she was totally justified in the work she was doing to make a better world, while relieving fools of their money and riding the planet of diseased creatures and non-vegetarians. According to Dr. Hazzard, she was doing the world a great service, and that kind of righteous determination makes the skin crawl.

When patients came to Dr. Hazzard, she began building trust, laying a foundation of promises to be fulfilled if they finished their treatments, and inflating the possible benefits of their health to the point that only an idiot would NOT want to do the treatment. Once they were psychologically conditioned to do only what she told them, and eat only what she provided, the patients were started on a tomato soup diet twice a day along with enemas. That's two cups of soup a day, for an adult body.

After the patients were significantly weakened, they were moved to an isolated location in Olalla where they would be unable to escape. There they were maintained on two cups of broth a day until they finally succumbed to death, but not before Linda appropriated everything they owned.

People came from all over the world to enroll in Linda Hazzard's health program, thanks in part to brilliant propaganda and a the human desperation for an answer to disease. People were willing to try anything, even fasting. Few, if any, knew of the fatality rate of Linda's sanitarium in the woods. After a time, the locals began to notice the goings on, but everyone assumed because these people had willingly come, they could willingly go.

One example of Linda's deeply controlling and evil state was to wait until the patient was delirious with hunger, as in Dora Williamson's case, then declare her insane and presume the responsibility of her guardianship, along with her medical treatment. As a guardian, Linda would then write checks to herself from Dora's account, as well as maintain that Dora could not leave Starvation Heights, effectively making her a prisoner of the island and of the treatment.

The sanitarium and Dr. Linda Hazzard claimed the lives of men, women, and even children. During the treatment reign of Dr. Hazzard, the body count became so high that Linda built a crematorium on the property to dispose of bodies locally, rather that ship them by ferry to Seattle.

There has also been speculation and gossip that the Butterworth funeral home was in league with Dr. Hazzard in so much as the bodies that she delivered were kept secret and the funeral prices—embalming and burials—were exorbitantly high in comparison to other less wealthy victims.

Eventually, Dr. Linda Hazzard was tried for the murder of Claire Williamson and found guilty. Although she did time for a couple of years, she returned to her practice upon her release and picked up where she left off in her work. To this day, no one knows exactly how many of her patients died under her "treatment," primarily because they were the wealthy patrons who went through the Butterworth and Sons funeral home, but there is speculation as to the number of unreported deaths due to the amount of poor and desperate people who went to Starvation Heights and were never seen again. There were also stories of parents who took their sick children for the cure and left them at the sanitarium, but never returned for them.

When Dr. Hazzard returned to Olalla following her incarceration, the sanitarium was completed and her patients increased exponentially, proof that even bad publicity is good publicity. Dr. Hazzard was her own last victim as she is reported to have died of starvation in June 1938.

Although the sanitarium burned to the ground shortly before her death, the home in which she and her family lived as well as several outbuildings remain. The resulting ghost stories of this property are intriguing as well as hair-raising. The family that resided in the house for twenty years grew up with spirits being a staple part of their child-hood.

On the list of deaths that are believed to be sure contributors to a haunting, starvation is actually in the top five. Decapitation, poison, dismemberment, and severe bodily trauma are also in the top five. So imagine for a moment, that thirty to forty people die of starvation on one piece of property… the spooky possibilities are endless.

The members of WSPIR went to Olalla to research this property and the following is some of the accounts that took place:

The first visit to Olalla, the two team psychics were blindfolded and the information about where they were going was kept secret so as not to influence them with the lore of the location. Everyone, psychics as well as ghost hunters, noted that the emotional weight of the energy was depressing and many of the members became irritable—"Ornery," "Cranky," and "Angry.". Yet upon leaving, they all felt immediately better.

On the second visit, WSPIR stayed the night, and at one point as they sat around the living room talking, someone said or did something that made the others laugh. What happened next is interesting because it seemed to catch…the laugh became almost a group mentality that spiraled out of control. Laughing erupted full scale till every member had tear streaked faces and surprised expressions. Each person to tell me the story said, "I've never laughed that hard in my life." Then as the group finally gave in, each person thinking, "I must have needed a good laugh." The psychics reported a void opening up in the ceiling, and a circling wind that sucked negative energy up through the roof and out of the home.

The non-psychic members didn't see or feel anything, but noted that almost immediately everyone stopped laughing at the same time, dried their eyes and looked around bewildered. The room didn't seem heavy anymore; the house appeared to have more light. While this phenomenon is not generally thought of as something that would be a ghost story per se, I believe it's worth mentioning simply because the event seemed to be out of the control of all those involved. I also believe it has merit in the realm of the search for the supernatural because the field as we know it is still infantile and growing. What we believe we know of energy and life after death is so miniscule that all information needs to be included. Therefore, a group mentality of something as simple as a laughing fit, especially in conjunction with the circumstance and location of a place is not, in my opinion, a fluke.

"It made me wonder when the last time that house had really heard any laughter," one woman said to me. Another reported, "I think we released something."

Everyone knows that laughter is medicine, and in a place that people went to die in search of health under the pseudo-care of Dr. Hazzard, it might have been the medicine that was so desperately needed these last ninety years. Joy is catharsis.

It's interesting to me that as I started the research for Starvation Heights, I had an extreme reaction to the material. While it's likely a psychosomatic response to the idea of starvation, I found myself almost constantly hungry. Often I would salivate at the mere idea of steak or a deep dish of mashed potatoes. It's worth noting that while I do eat these foods, I can't say when I've been so excited to eat. Again, it might be nothing more than the psychological backlash of researching the evil intentions of a "fasting specialist" but I think it's strange enough to include. One day, as I decided I really needed to finish reading Starvation Heights, I said to my friend, "I have to finish this book today, because it's doing terrible things to my weight!"

I ate a hearty lunch and sat down on the sofa next to him while he played video games and I read. I couldn't have read more than a chapter before my stomach began to grumble. After a half hour or so of apologizing for every growl and moan coming from my belly, he set his game down and said, "Just eat something already!"

"I just ate!" I whined, "I just ate a huge lunch!"

I can say with a comical grin as I write this that I am so relieved to be done working on this story. Dr. Linda Hazzard and her story of murder and starvation struck a strong sympathetic chord that I'd be more than happy to never revisit.

Butterworth Mortuary

Seattle's first mortuary at 1921 First Ave. is now occupied by a nightclub and a popular Irish pub. The four story structure was built to accommodate the burial needs of the downtown area.

The back opens up to Post Alley and housed the stables and the embalming room, whereas the front, which maintains a beautiful entrance on First, is now a posh bar. In the days of the morgue, the front would have housed the chapel and stairs to the upper floor for the mortician's household.

I began my search in the front. According to Jake, the clubs and bars that have made a home in the front have been short lived and rarely successful. I decided to stop in before the evening rush on a Friday night. I didn't plan on any serious investigating, hoping instead to ask a few questions of the staff, enjoy a cup of coffee, and test the atmosphere. The exterior of the building is a façade of grey castle stonework and red brick, and the original tiles at the entrance are still in place. The artistic hexagon pieces are indicative of the decorative craftsmanship of the era at the turn of the twentieth century and I found it a little unnerving to be walking over the threshold which says, "CHAPEL" in bold letters and shows a mural on the wall nearby of the original Butterworth estate in England. Perhaps it was my imagination but it felt like stepping over a grave.

Sitting at the bar I ordered a coffee—six thirty and there wasn't a pot brewed.

"I'm sorry; we usually don't get orders for coffee till late. I'll go brew a pot." The blonde bartender was tall and pretty, the sort of fashionable beauty that seemed to grow on trees in the greater Seattle area.

"No worries," I said. "Could I ask you a few questions while it's brewing?"

ER Butterworth's and Sons is now Starlite Lounge.

Original chapel tiles at the Starlite Lounge entrance.

She glanced at the only other person at the bar, a stocky guy with short black hair and a goatee. He flipped through a newspaper without looking up. "Sure. I'll be right back."

When she returned and bustled behind the counter, arranging glasses and filling the straw holders, I asked, "So how long have you guys been open?"

"A few months." She didn't seem eager to talk.

"How's business?"

She looked at me, "Okay. We usually get busy around nine."

I was getting the very distinct impression that she didn't really want to be talking to me. I wondered if it was me or if perhaps she was just having a bad day. Aren't bartenders supposed to be all friendly and sociable?

She excused herself to go get the coffee, so I decided to have a look around. Black and russet walls and twelve-foot ceilings topped with white crown molding were accented by red velvet couches and stainless steel barstools with black leather seats. All the decorations down to the wall mural of famous Jazz icons behind the bar had a newness to it that verified the place hadn't seriously been broken in yet as a high profile lounge.

She returned with my coffee and I climbed back onto my barstool squeaking the leather with my jeans. The coffee came in a glass mug, the kind usually used to serve Irish coffees. The sugar packets were hard and I didn't bother asking for cream. There was certainly an unwelcome feeling. So much for polite conversation, it was time for a more serious approach.

I pulled my notebook and pen from my bag.

"Did you know this place used to be a mortuary?" I asked.

She shook her head and glanced at the other guy at the end of the bar.

"Have any weird or unexplainable things happened since you started working here?"

She shook her head again. I wondered how old she was – twenty two, maybe twenty-four.

"Do you know how I can contact of the owner of the business? Maybe a card or a phone number?" I took a sip of my coffee. It was the first and last drink I'd try—it tasted as though they'd used old gym socks for the filter. The bartender gave me a card and turned to leave.

"I'm gathering research for a book on ghosts. Is there anyone who works here who might be interested in talking to me?" I was starting to feel a little desperate, my first big writing gig and I wasn't even able to get a bartender to talk. Clearly, I was doing something wrong.

She motioned to the guy sitting at the bar with the paper, "Tony works here, too. He'd be the one you want to talk with." She left with an air that I felt like, 'I've done all I can. Your turn, Tony.'

Tony looked at me over the classifieds. While I wasn't intimidated, I certainly wasn't feeling a sense of enthusiasm wafting off of him.

"So, have you seen anything weird since you've been here?"

He shrugged and I realized, based on his size and dark clothes—he must be the bouncer. Great. So much for the hospitality.

"Not really," he said. "Sometimes bottles fall off the shelf back there." He pointed at the shelf below the Jazz mural behind the bar.

I perked up. "Really?"

He folded the paper slowly, and for a second I thought of a club owner from the '40s sitting down the mahogany from me with a fat cigar and an offer I couldn't refuse. Okay, so I was starting to feel intimidated.

"Yeah." Abruptly his demeanor changed, he had a willing audience. Perhaps fearful and curious, but an audience. "Sometimes the girls get uncomfortable around closing time."

"Like the heebie-jeebies?" I asked.

"I guess, yeah." Turning on his stool toward me, Tony rested a large hand on his knee. "Not like their scared or anything, just, you know—uneasy."

"Sure," I agreed.

"Sometimes there's weird sounds at night," he added.

"Sounds like what?"

"Footsteps. That kind of thing. And right after we moved in here… the shelves in the back—the ones we installed—collapsed. Twice."

"Huh," I murmured. "That's very interesting." I suddenly didn't buy any of it. Call it the skeptical bubble, but I distinctly felt as though I were being hammed.

"But that's about it." Tony turned back to his paper. The window of opportunity vanished and I sat quietly alone at the bar—the bartender was still nowhere to be found. After scribbling down my notes I said goodnight to Tony, left money next to my once-touched coffee and made off toward Post Alley, where the other half of the building housed the famous Irish pub, Kell's.

Walking down Post Alley, half a block from the market, I could almost envision the way things used to be, when Seattle was an infant city. New stone buildings were rising from the ashes of the 1889 fire, the social structure still held wobbles from power struggles, and the acceptance of Statehood; but the economic backbone would have been building strength before the depression of 1893. Post Alley is where the stables and servant entrances were to the beautiful houses that faced Front Street, and because only the wealthy could afford a house on Front Street, the stables and servant entrances by default were beautiful.

Kell's is proudly marked by an Irish flag on the red brick Victorian walls of the old Mortuary. At a quarter after seven, the dinner rush was still in full swing. I found a table in the back in sight of the bartender to wait for one of the owners. When I'd called earlier, the waitress told me that is was best just to show up, as the owners hung out all day, and it would be better for me to talk to them in person. The bartender told me on arrival that the

owner had just stepped out, but that he'd be back shortly and I could just wait. So I did.

Kell's Irish Pub once housed the stable and embalming area for the Butterworth Mortuary.

It took nearly a half hour to catch the eye of the waitress for a cup of coffee, thankfully much better than the last cup I'd just had. Then I waited. The interior of the bar is a rich golden wood, brass, and walls of black and white photographs. The atmosphere was warm and inviting so I pulled out my sketch journal and kept myself busy for the next three hours. Periodically, I'd check with the bartender but he seemed embarrassed, "I'm sorry, he's usually here by now."

I ordered dinner and continued to doodle. By eleven I was getting tired and sore from sitting, so I decided to call it a night. Outside, the evening was warm, the scent of the ocean soaking the heavy air with fish, salt, and seaweed. A little cranky, I was feeling like a bit of a failure—after all, what sort of detective was I turning out to be; I had nothing. I dug in my bag for my emergency pack of Clove cigarettes, reserved only for really bad days.

I smoked on the way back to my Jeep, and decided that for my first non-fiction book, I wasn't doing so great. Although I wasn't doing terrible yet, either. Making a few mental notes on what not to do next time, I drove back to the house singing at the top of my lungs. You win some, and lose some, right? Tomorrow would be better.

I turned to the Seattle Ghosts Hunters again, who had a wealth of stories for me.

The first pertained to the Starlite Lounge, formerly known as Fire and Ice. They confirmed stories of footsteps. They also told me that there have been problems reported with the electric appliances, tools moving from one location to another, and disco lights. While there was, at one time, a disco ball in the early days of the lounge, the reported lights were not reflective of the time period.

The best story they told me, though, was of the reoccurring apparition of a woman seen from the waist up. In her appearances, she has never had legs, but the upper half of her body is evidently costumed in a "very conservative" turn of the century high-collar blouse. Her hair is in a bun and she wanders through the building.

Joe Teeples told me that, as he was speaking with a man at the lounge, he had his back turned to the hallway when the man's face went white and he froze mid-sentence. Joe turned around to see what had spooked his friend, but there was nothing there. The friend later reported having sighted the upper body of a turn-of-the-century woman floating by.

During the remodel of the lounge space, one construction worker stood on a ladder while attempting to adjust a light fixture. He glanced over and saw a table with two strange men, but didn't think much of it until, out of the corner of his eye, he saw a woman walk past them. When he heard the men shouting abusive language at the woman, the construction worker turned in anger toward them and saw the woman was present only from the waist up, whereupon he blinked and did a double take; when he looked back, the two men and the woman were gone.

Another account tells of a group of men sitting at a table after closing when a full bottle of wine floated off the shelf near the bar and drifted on thin air out the open door,where it dropped to the sidewalk without breaking. Needless to say, the conversation halted immediately and the comfortable mood of evening conversation was shattered.

One woman I had a chance to interview, Missy, had an experience at the Starlite Lounge that convinced her that the space was indeed haunted.

"They'd been open for a couple of months and I went in before it got busy. I was sitting at one end of the bar, and the bartender was facing away when a shot glass down the way slid off the shelf and landed on the floor with a thump. The bartender turned and looked at me but I was so astonished—it did it right in front of me all by itself. Then she walked over to the shelf and put it back up there. It didn't break, it was that heavy glass, you know. Then she turned around and it did it again!"

Missy is convinced that the Starlite is haunted.

When I asked if Seattle Ghost Hunters had heard anything about Kell's, Joe told me he'd gone in to talk to the owner one day. He set an EMF detector on the table during the interview. As they talked a young mother and her daughter were having lunch a few tables over. The child refused to remain seated and kept running to the back of the main dining area near hall. The mother was clearly agitated and embarrassed that the child wouldn't simply sit and eat, and finally in a fit of frustration, caught the girl and asked, "Where do you keep running off to? Sit down and eat."

The girl, between five and seven years of age replied, "I'm playing with the girl back there."

The EMF detector suddenly "went nuts" and investigation into the back of the room and the hall revealed no other living souls, or confirmations of ghosts.

After researching the story of Starvation Heights, the rumor of connections between the murders in Olalla, committed by Dr. Linda Hazzard, and the haunting in Kell's and The Starlite Lounge are entirely possible. Someone even told me they thought the primary reason restaurants rarely stayed open for more than a year in area of Starlight Lounge is because the ghosts that haunt the place died of starvation, therefore, they are drawn to the food and drive away the business. Obviously, I can't say whether this is true or not, but the very fact that it was mentioned is an interesting curiosity that shows a great deal about the mentality and acceptance of the local ghost lore.

Kell's and The Starlite Lounge are fantastic examples of the way Seattle residents treat their legends; a little respect, a dash of reverence, an open mind and a hearty dose of humor.

Georgetown Castle

One of the more infamous haunted locations of Seattle is the George-town Castle. Over what has been a colorful history of the home; includ-ing its days as a gambling lodge, a brothel, a prohibition storehouse, a Masonic meeting location, an artists studio, and of course a much loved home, this three story house has seen its share of brutality and ghosts.

In the early days of Seattle's conception, the southern outskirts of the city is where the questionable activity, or vices were housed; drinking, gambling, and prostitution. Georgetown, as it was named, became the cesspool of the burgeoning new empire of the Pacific Northwest. Most of the houses of the period have since been replaced, but many remain that show the typical Victorian and Craftsman architectural embellish-ments and beauty that is a much desired esthetics in the current housing market. This is the story of the Georgetown Castle.

The first time I saw the Castle in late May 2006, I was not so very im-pressed. The exterior was bland and while the structure of the building seemed to have elegance, the outside was clearly in need of fixing. That, how-ever, only enhanced the ambiance as Jake told stories of the hauntings.

There are many reports of the usual paranormal phenomena; foot-steps, voices, and slammed doors, but the Castle also has a few more interesting specters.

One story I heard repeated three times from separate sources goes like this: Once, there was a visitor to the Castle in the 1980s who had no knowledge of the unusual events. He evidently could not sleep and walked down the stairs to the kitchen in the middle of the night. Because he was a visitor, he didn't feel terribly comfortable rooting through the cupboards for food, but he was hungry. "I wonder where they keep the bread?" he mumbled to himself. Then, from across the room, a loaf of bread emerged from a cupboard and rolled across the table top to rest in front of him.

The Georgetown Castle.

The sources that delighted in telling me the story seemed to think the helpful ghost was Sarah. Sarah has been spotted on several occasions in turn-of-the-century garb with long dark hair. In fact, there is a persistent rumor that the artist who bought the Castle, witnessed the ethereal form of Sarah on a frequent basis. It's also claimed that she sat for a portrait that was painted by one of the artsy owners, whereupon the portrait was hung on the landing of the second floor. The painting has long since disappeared, and the house sold to new owners.

It's interesting enough to me to note that the Castle is underneath the flight path of the Boeing airfield. While I can't reasonably see a connection to the events of Georgetown and the Castle in particular, it's important to understand that during the ninety years that Boeing has been testing planes and building the fleets that carry passengers all over the world, there have been a handful of very deadly plane crashes in this area.

Mostly, they are attributed to the testing phases of new engineering, but the fact remains that when a test plane goes down on the flight path near Georgetown, the population is dense enough that the resulting crash inevitably takes a couple dozen innocent bystanders with it.

November 3, 1937, two planes collide over Boeing field. Five men die.

February 18, 1943, the top secret XB-29 prototype Superfortress takes off from Boeing field on a test run. Twenty minutes later the plane crashes into Frye's meat packing plant killing the eleven men on board and nineteen workers at the meat plant.

January 2, 1949, an airliner carrying Yale students crashes at Boeing field killing three crewmembers and eleven students.

July 19, 1949, an airliner crashes in Georgetown killing two passengers, five citizens, and injuring thirty-nine others as it destroys seven houses.

August 13, 1951, a B-50 Bomber takes off from Boeing field and develops engine trouble before glancing off Sick's Seattle Brewing and Malting Company. It crashes into the Lester Apartments located on Beacon Hill. Interestingly, the Lester Apartments was once the most infamous brothel in Seattle housing 500 rooms. The crash claimed the lives of six crewmen and five citizens and injured a dozen more. It's nothing less than miraculous that more lives weren't lost in this crash.

While there are more fatal crashes through the history of Boeing airfield, the point is that the Georgetown is near these traumatic events.

Among the lore surrounding the Castle, there exists a convoluted tale of a lover's triangle. The way I heard it told maintained that one of the first couples to own the house brought the younger sister of the woman to live with them from the East Coast after her parents died. The young woman moved in with the couple, and it wasn't long before the girl became pregnant. While versions differ as to whether the girl was raped or entered a relationship with her much older brother-in law willingly, the outcome is the same. The girl gives birth to a child whereupon the man murders the child and buries it under the front porch.

Sounds of a woman crying, phantom arguments, and moaning have been reported. As well as a sighting of an old woman who chokes herself with one hand and slaps at witnesses with the other.

The Seattle Ghost Hunters, headed by AJ, obtained permission to study Georgetown Castle on August 5, 2006. They were gracious enough to share with me the information they collected.

Seattle Ghost Hunters reported "random keying" of the walkie-talkies (when the walkie-talkie picks up a click or a beep like someone on the other end is trying to make contact). This was mostly attributed to the nearness of Boeing Airfield—except for the instance when the team heard a very distinct "Hello" over the waves. The upstairs team then radioed the downstairs team, but everyone holding a radio denied having said "Hello."

The team experienced a temperature drop of a few degrees in the kitchen. Several team members also heard a little girl on the third floor stairs whispering and singing "London Bridge."

They documented orb activity and EMF anomalies. During the investigation, the team also heard an audible sigh. Two of the members of Seattle Ghost Hunters are psychic investigators. During the visit to the Castle, the psychics reported children on the third floor. One psychic picked up the tale of a man pushing his pregnant girlfriend down the stairs. And at yet another time, the impression of a man covered in blood stood near the team. Psychics also confirmed the presence of a child spirit under the porch. Violence has been an unfortunate part of the Castle's history.

When the team wrapped up their investigation at 3:20 am, two of the female members mentioned they were quite happy to leave the house, as they didn't feel welcome.

The second time I returned to the Castle, three months had lapsed. The Castle's current ownership is new and vibrant and very much in harmony with the spiritual ancestry of the building. The exterior paint had been redone; the wrap-around porch under remodel and the interior of the building is undergoing a complete refurbish. As I stood at the door talking to one of the owners, I was surprised by the transformation that had taken place in a mere three months. The colors alone brightened the atmosphere from dreary and spooky to a glowing place of welcome. While it's still unfinished, the difference was spectacular. The new owners were also going to great lengths to ensure that the house maintained as much of its originality and features as possible. I was pleased to note that the craftsman woodwork was being painted rather than replaced. I've been told that a remodel or a renovation will often stir up entities that were otherwise sleeping, so I would be interested to know what the house spirits are like upon the completion of the Castle.

AJ related a funny story to me that the new owner told her. In one of the bathrooms, the owner had put new decorations; one of these was an orange bathmat. Every time the owner came into the bathroom the bathmat would be twisted, or folded, or scrunched up. Each time she saw it, the owner would straighten it out, line it up with the tub, and leave. One time she became suspicious, and fixed the mat, then left and closed the bathroom door, waiting in the hall for a moment before opening the door to find the mat askew.

One day, she fixed the mat and went to the kitchen only to return and find the mat wadded up in the tub and soaking wet. She replaced the "ugly orange bathmat" that day, and since has had no problems. Evidently, the ghost has preferences or at least a strong sense of home decorating fashion.

I also found it amusing that the psychics picked up a thought from the spectral residents about an alter in the home to the Lady of Guadeloupe. The Latin influence of the new owners could very well be the reason the home is being treated with so much respect and in sync with the residents of the afterlife. Culturally, the Latin beliefs of honoring spirits and respecting the dead differ greatly from the current American culture.

Personally, I think the Latin approach is much healthier and a lot more fun. When the psychics picked up disgruntled spiritual commentary about the alter, the psychic replied to the spirits. "Get over it. They're here to stay."

I didn't get a chance to walk through the castle myself—a disappointment, but also understandable being that it is a home. The restoration project, even between the few months I saw the house from the outside and from the front door looking in, was spectacular.

Conclusion

Jake ended her tour in the parking lot of the Center for Wooden Boats. As the van pulled to a stop and passengers shuffled through their bags, she asked, "So I'll ask you once again before you head home for the night... Who here on this tour believes in ghosts?"

The couple in the back still agreed with enthusiasm, the family in the center shrugged again and when Jake's grey eyes came to rest on my face, I smiled. "I think I'm still on the fence."

She shrugged with a good-natured, *no hard feelings, but I did my best* sort of movement and smiled. "You will some day."

I wasn't sure what to make of that as I walked back to my jeep and headed for the freeway. I wondered what exactly would make me believe in ghosts. I realized then, as I passed Seattle, waking to the night life and city glow of a Friday evening, I didn't actually NOT believe in ghosts—I just didn't believe in them as they are portrayed in the hype of stories, as moaning spirits in torn bed sheets.

Skyscrapers lit the edges of the freeway as I blasted music on my way down I-5 and determined that, *Yes, I actually am a believer*—but to say this it requires a redefinition of the term "ghost" for me. I believe in *something*, but as of yet there is no pop culture explanation, or scientific proof, or even a semi-logical label that is applicable. As I drove home from my haunted tour of Seattle, I decided to work on my theory about the paranormal.

During my research of Seattle ghosts, I'd had my fair share of the heebie-jeebies, the sense of being watched or not alone, times when I was mildly uncomfortable, and at least one Hitchcock moment when a bird in an alley made me squeak. I'd been covered in spider webs, hit with the chills, hands and knees covered in dust from crawling around, and blistered feet. I thought I was losing my mind more than once, but most strongly when I came back from a shower to discover my bed made. My room mates wouldn't fess up to it, so it left me with a creepy sense of either being toyed with—or the very real possibility that exhaustion and imagination were winning a battle of the wits. I cannot say with conviction that I encountered a spirit, entity or even a presence, but doubt has firmly lodged itself in my psyche, which was cause enough to explore my feelings on the subject matter after four months of sleuthing.

I believe that people are energetic. That we are a source of water and power, and when we die, that current remains and is capable of affecting those we leave behind. I think that the stronger we are as living beings, the stronger the ripple that echoes behind us. I believe there is a realm we are currently unable to explore because we lack the scientific advancement, and the spiritual flexibility. I can't say whether the supernatural, as we might think of it, exists in the paradoxal equations of Quantum Mechanics or if it's as simple as a leap of human imagination.

What I can say, though, is whether or not spirits haunt the living, we as people are fascinated, terrified, and intrigued by the idea of life after death. Our very existence is permeated with the knowledge of mortality and we fixate on death and dying as a part of our living experience. Knowing this, we can play on our fear, and enjoy the torment of stories around the campfire, and scream fests at the theatre. We fork out cash for the latest big screen thriller and curl up at night careful not to let our toes dangle over the edge of the bed. Paranormal or imagination, this phenomenon is a colorful and entertaining aspect of our culture and I feel it should be embraced. Real or imagined.

The residents of Seattle love their ghosts. They boast with pride about the convoluted history of violence and tragedy. They sit with strangers over a drink at a bar and repeat in theatrical whispers, the gruesome details of murder and intrigue that make their beloved city a great place to explore the realm of spirits. Seattle welcomes all visitors, be they spectral or the next town over. The dedicated ghost hunters of the area and the boisterous tour guides invite you to join them, come see for yourself.

Pull up a chair, put a marshmallow on a stick, and see for yourself if you will walk away believing in ghosts.

Seattle from the Space Needle.

* The following section is provided by the Chester County Paranormal Research Society in Pennsylvania and appears in training materials for new investigators. Though many of these terms are not discussed in this book, they may be of assistance to you, should you decide to delve further into the great unknown.

Please visit www.chestercountyprs.com for more information.

Glossary and Equipment Explanations

Air Probe Thermometer
A thermometer with an external probe that is capable of taking instant measurements of the air temperature.

Anomalous field
A field that can not be explained or ruled out by various possibilities, that can be a representation of spirit or paranormal energy present.

Apparition
A transparent form of a human or animal, a spirit.

Artificial field
A field that is caused by electrical outlets, appliances, etc.

Aural Enhancer
A listening device that enhances or amplifies audio signals. i.e., Orbitor Bionic Ear.

Automatic writing
The act of a spirit guiding a human agent in writing a message that is brought through by the spirit.

Base readings
The readings taken at the start of an investigation and are used as a means of comparing other readings taken later during the course of the investigation.

Demonic Haunting
A haunting that is caused by an inhuman or subhuman energy or spirit.

Dowsing Rods
A pair of L-shaped rods or a single Y-shaped rod, used to detect the presence of what the person using them is trying to find.

Electro-static generator
    A device that electrically charges the air often used in paranormal investigations/research as a means to contribute to the materialization of paranormal or spiritual energy.

ELF
    Extremely Low Frequency.

ELF Meter/EMF Meter
    A device that measures electric and magnetic fields.

EMF
    Electro Magnetic Field.

EVP
    Electronic Voice Phenomena.

False positive
    Something that is being interpreted as paranormal within a picture or video and is, in fact, a natural occurrence or defect of the equipment used.

Gamera
    A 35mm film camera connected with a motion detector that is housed in a weather proof container and takes a picture when movement is detected. Made by Silver Creek Industries.

Geiger Counter
    A device that measures gamma and x-ray radiation.

Infra Red
    An invisible band of radiation at the lower end of the visible light spectrum. With wavelengths from 750 nm to 1 mm, infrared starts at the end of the microwave spectrum and ends at the beginning of visible light. Infrared transmission typically requires an unobstructed line of sight between transmitter and receiver. Widely used in most audio and video remote controls, infrared transmission is also used for wireless connections between computer devices and a variety of detectors.

Intelligent haunting
    A haunting of a spirit or other entity that has the ability to interact with the living and do things that can make its presence known.

Milli-gauss
Unit of measurement, measures in 1000th of a gauss and is named for the famous German mathematician, Karl Gauss.

Orbs
Anomalous spherical shapes that appear on video and still photography.

Pendulum
A pointed item that is hung on the end of a string or chain and is used as a means of contacting spirits. An individual will hold the item and let it hang from the finger tips. The individual will ask questions aloud and the pendulum answers by moving.

Poltergeist haunting
A haunting that has two sides, but same kinds of activity in common. Violent outbursts of activity with doors and windows slamming shut, items being thrown across a room and things being knocked off of surfaces. Poltergeist hauntings are usually focused around a specific individual who resides or works at the location of the activity reported, and, in some cases, when the person is not present at the location, activity does not occur. A poltergeist haunting may be the cause of a human agent or spirit/energy that may be present at the location.

Portal
An opening in the realm of the paranormal that is a gateway between one dimension and the next. A passageway for spirits to come and go through. See also Vortex.

Residual haunting
A haunting that is an imprint of an event or person that plays itself out like a loop until the energy that causes it has burned itself out.

Scrying
The act of eliciting information with the use of a pendulum from spirits.

Table Tipping
A form of spirit communication, the act of a table being used as a form of contact. Individuals will sit around a table and lightly place there fingertips on the edge of the table and elicit contact with a spirit. The Spirit will respond by "tipping" or moving the table.

Talking Boards
A board used as a means of communicating with a spirit. Also known as a Quija Board.

Vortex
A place or situation regarded as drawing into its center all that surrounds it.

White Noise
A random noise signal that has the same sound energy level at all frequencies.

In this section, the Chester County Paranormal Research Society looks at the application and benefits of equipment used on investigations with greater detail. The equipment used for an investigation plays a vital role in the ability to collect objective evidence and helps to determine what *is* and *is not* paranormal activity. But a key point to be made here is: the investigator is the most important tool on any investigation. With that said, let us now take a look at the main pieces of equipment used during an investigation...

The Geiger Counter
The Geiger counter is device that measures radiation. A "Geiger counter" usually contains a metal tube with a thin metal wire along its middle. The space in between them is sealed off and filled with a suitable gas and with the wire at about +1000 volts relative to the tube.

An ion or electron penetrating the tube (or an electron knocked out of the wall by X-rays or gamma rays) tears electrons off atoms in the gas. Because of the high positive voltage of the central wire, those electrons are then attracted to it. They gain energy that collide with atoms and release more electrons, until the process snowballs into an "avalanche", producing an easily detectable pulse of current. With a suitable filling gas, the flow of electricity stops by itself, or else the electrical circuitry can help stop it.

The instrument was called a "counter" because every particle passing it produced an identical pulse, allowing particles to be counted, usually electronically. But it did not tell anything about their identity or energy, except that they must have sufficient energy to penetrate the walls of the counter.

The Geiger counter is used in paranormal research to measure the background radiation at a location. The working theory in this field is that paranormal activity can effect the background radiation. In some cases, it will increase the radiation levels and in other cases it will decrease the levels.

Digital and 35mm Film Cameras

The camera is an imperative piece of equipment that enabled us to gather objective evidence during a case. Some of the best evidence presented from cases of paranormal activity over the years has been because of photographs taken. If you own your own digital camera or 35mm film camera, you need to be fully aware of what the cameras abilities and limitations are. Digital cameras have been at the center of great debate in the field of paranormal research over the years.

The earlier incarnations of digital cameras were full of inherent problems and notorious for creating "false positive" pictures. A "false positive" picture is a picture that has anomalous elements within the picture that are the result of a camera defect or other natural occurrence. There are many pictures scattered about the internet that claim to be of true paranormal activity, but in fact they are "false positives." Orbs, defined as anomalous paranormal energy that can show up as balls of light or streaks in still photography or video, are the most controversial pictures of paranormal energy in the field. There are so many theories (good and bad) about the origin of orbs and what they are. Every picture in the CCPRS collection that has an orb—or orbs—are not presented in a way that state that they are absolutely paranormal of nature. I have yet to capture an orb photo that made me feel certain that in fact it is of a paranormal nature.

If you use your own camera, understand that your camera is vital. I encourage all members who own their own cameras to do research on the make and model of the camera and see what other consumers are saying about them. Does the manufacturer give any info regarding possible defects or design flaws with that particular model? Understanding your camera will help to rule out the possibility of interpreting a "false positive" for an authentic picture of paranormal activity.

Video Cameras

The video camera is also a fundamental tool in the investigation as another way for collecting objective evidence that can support the proof of paranormal activity. The video camera can be used in various ways during the investigation. It can be set on a tripod and left in a location where paranormal activity has been reported. It can also be used as a hand-held camera and the investigator will take it with them during their walk through investigation as a means of documenting to hopefully capture anomalous activity on tape. Infra-Red technology has become a feature on most consumer level video cameras and depending on the manufacturer can be called "night shot" or "night alive." What this technology does is allow us to use the camera in zero light. Most cameras with this feature will add a green tint or haze to the camera when it is being used in this mode. A video camera with this ability holds great appeal to the paranormal investigator.

EMF/ELF Meters

EMF=Electro Magnetic Frequency   ELF=Extremely Low Frequency

What is an EMF/ELF meter? Good question. The EMF/ELF meter is a meter that measures Electric and Magnetic fields in an AC or DC current field. It measures in a unit of measurement called "milli-gauss," named for the famous German mathematician, Karl Gauss. Most meters will measure in a range of 1-5 or 1-10 milli-gauss. The reason that EMF meters are used in paranormal research is because of the theory that a spirit or paranormal energy can add to the energy field when it is materializing or is present in a location. The theory says that, typically, an energy that measures between 3-7 milli-gauss may be of a paranormal origin. This doesn't mean that an artificial field can't also measure within this range. That is why we take base readings and make maps notating where artificial fields occur. The artificial fields are a direct result of electricity, i.e. wiring, appliances, light switches, electrical outlets, circuit breakers, high voltage power lines, sub-stations, etc.

The Earth emits a naturally occurring magnetic field all around us and has an effect on paranormal activity. Geo-magnetic storm activity can also have a great influence on paranormal activity. For more information on this kind of phenomena visit: www.noaa.sec.com.

There are many different types of EMF meters; and each one, although it measures with the same unit of measurement, may react differently. An EMF meter can range from anywhere to $12.00 to $1,000.00 or more depending on the quality and features that it has. Most meters are measuring the AC (alternating current, the type of fields created by man-made electricity) fields and some can measure DC (direct current-naturally occurring fields, batteries also fall into the category of DC) fields. The benefit of having a meter that can measure DC fields is that they will automatically filter out the artificial fields created by AC fields and can pick up more naturally occurring electro magnetic fields. Some of the higher-tech EMF meters are so sensitive that they can pick up the fields generated by living beings. The EMF meter was originally designed to measure the earth's magnetic fields and also to measure the fields created by electrical an artificial means.

There have been various studies over the years about the long term effects of individuals living in or near high fields. There has been much controversy as to whether or not long term exposure to high fields can lead to cancer. It has been proven though that no matter what, long term exposure to high fields can be harmful to your health. The ability to locate these high fields within a private residence or business is vital to the investigation. We may offer suggestions to the client as to possible solutions for dealing with high fields. The wiring in a home or business can greatly affect the possibility of high fields. If the wiring is old and/or not shielded correctly, it can emit high fields that may affect the ability to correctly notate any anomalous fields that may be present.

Audio Recording Equipment

Audio recording equipment is used for conducting EVP (Electronic Voice Phenomena) research and experiments. What is an EVP? An EVP is a phenomenon where paranormal voices or sounds can be captured with audio recording devices. The theory is that the activity will imprint directly onto the device or tape, but has not been proven to be an absolute fact. The use of an external microphone is essential when conducting EVP experiments with analog recording equipment. The internal microphone on an analog tape recorder can pick up the background noise of the working parts within the tape recorder and can taint the evidence as a whole. Most digital recorders are quiet enough to use the internal microphone, but as a general rule of thumb, we do not use them. An external microphone will be used always. Another theory about EVP research is that an authentic EVP will happen within the range 250-400hz. This is a lower frequency range and isn't easily heard by the human ear, and the human voice does not emit in this range. EVP is rarely heard at the moment it happens—it is usually revealed during the playback and analysis portion of the investigation.

Thermometers

The use of a thermometer in an investigation goes without saying. This is how we monitor the temperature changes during the course of an investigation. CCPRS is currently using Digital thermometers with remote sensors as a way to set up a perimeter and to notate any changes in a stationary location of an investigation. The Air-probe thermometer can take "real time" readings that are instantly accurate. This is the more appropriate thermometer for measuring air temperature and "cold spots" that may be caused by the presence of paranormal phenomena. The IR Non-contact thermometer is the most misused thermometer in the field of paranormal research. CCPRS does not own or use IR Non-contact thermometers for this reason. The IR (infra-red) Non-contact thermometer is meant for measuring surface temperatures from a remote location. It shoots an infrared beam out to an object and bounces to the unit and gives the temperature reading. I have seen, first hand, investigators using this thermometer as a way to measure air temperature. NO, this is not correct! Enough said. In an email conversation that I have had with Grant Wilson from TAPS, he has said that, "Any change in temperature that can't be measured with your hand is not worth notating…"

Bibliography
and Other Resources

Allison, Ross and Joe Teeples. *Ghostology 101: Becoming a Ghost Hunter*. AuthorHouse, Bloomington, IN, 2005.

Crowley, Walt & The HistoryLink Staff. *HistoryLink's Seattle & King County Timeline*. Litho Craft Inc., Lynwood, WA, 2001.

Drew, Kim; Michael Yaeger & Sheila Lyon. "Know Your Pike Place Market Ghosts." Publisher/Date Unknown.

Evans, Jack R. *Little History of Pike Place Market*. SCW Publications, Seattle, WA, 1991.

Olsen, Gregg. *Starvation Heights*. Three Rivers Press, New York, NY, 1997.

Smith, Barbara. *Ghost Stories of Washington*. Lone Pine Publishing, Auburn, WA, 2000.

Websites

http://www.Historylink.org
http://www.aghost.us/index.html
http://www.privateeyetours.com/
http://www.wspir.com/index.htm
http://www.seattleghosthunters.com/
http://hauntedhouses.com/states/wa/
http://www.legendsofamerica.com/WA-PikeMarket.htm
http://www.beliefnet.com/

My greatest resources were the friendly citizens of Seattle.